The Crypto Profit Playbook

Discipline Disciple

Published by Discipline Disciple, 2024.

While every precaution has been taken in the preparation of this book, the publisher assumes no responsibility for errors or omissions, or for damages resulting from the use of the information contained herein.

THE CRYPTO PROFIT PLAYBOOK

First edition. July 16, 2024.

ISBN: 979-8227173782

Written by Discipline Disciple.

Table of Contents

Introduction

Welcome and Purpose

Welcome to **The Crypto Profit Playbook**. In a world where digital assets are rapidly becoming mainstream, understanding the intricacies of cryptocurrency investment is crucial. This ebook is designed to be your comprehensive guide, leading you through the complex yet rewarding landscape of cryptocurrencies. Whether you are a novice taking your first steps into the crypto world or an experienced investor looking to refine your strategies, this book aims to equip you with the essential knowledge and tools to maximise your profits.

Cryptocurrencies, underpinned by blockchain technology, represent a revolutionary shift in how we think about money, investments, and the transfer of value. The rise of Bitcoin and other cryptocurrencies has opened a myriad of opportunities for investors, but it has also introduced a significant level of risk and uncertainty. The volatile nature of this market can be daunting, but with the right strategies and a disciplined approach, it is possible to navigate these challenges successfully.

The primary goal of this ebook is to demystify the world of cryptocurrency investing. We will start with the basics, ensuring you have a solid understanding of what cryptocurrencies are, how they work, and why they matter. From there, we will delve into a variety of profit-making strategies, each tailored to different levels of risk tolerance and investment styles. Whether you are interested in long-term holding, active trading, or passive income opportunities, you will find detailed guidance to help you make informed decisions.

One of the key themes of this book is risk management. In any form of investing, but especially in the volatile world of cryptocurrencies, managing risk is paramount. We will explore various techniques to protect your investments, including diversification, setting stop-loss orders, and staying informed about market trends. By the end of this book, you will have a toolkit of strategies to not only seek profits but also to mitigate potential losses.

In addition to practical investment strategies, this ebook will provide insights into the broader ecosystem of cryptocurrencies. This includes understanding the regulatory landscape, recognising potential scams, and evaluating new projects and technologies. The aim is to empower you to make decisions based on knowledge and critical thinking, rather than speculation or hype.

As you embark on this journey, remember that the world of cryptocurrency is constantly evolving. What works today might change tomorrow, and staying adaptable is key. This ebook is not just a static guide but a foundation upon which you can build your knowledge and adapt to the ever-changing crypto landscape. Let **The Crypto Profit Playbook** be your companion in navigating this exciting and often unpredictable market, helping you to achieve your financial goals and maximise your potential in the world of digital assets.

Importance of Cryptocurrency

Cryptocurrency has emerged as one of the most significant technological innovations of the 21st century, fundamentally altering the landscape of finance and digital ownership. To appreciate its importance, it is essential to understand its brief yet impactful history and the role it plays in today's economy.

The concept of cryptocurrency was first introduced in 2008 with the publication of a whitepaper titled "Bitcoin: A Peer-to-Peer Electronic

Cash System" by an unknown person or group of people using the pseudonym Satoshi Nakamoto. Bitcoin aimed to create a decentralised digital currency that would allow transactions without the need for a central authority, such as a bank or government. This decentralisation is achieved through blockchain technology, a public ledger that records all transactions transparently and immutably.

Bitcoin's launch in 2009 marked the beginning of a new era in digital finance. Initially, it garnered interest primarily from technologists and libertarians who were intrigued by its potential to disrupt traditional financial systems. However, as its value began to increase, and more people recognised its potential, Bitcoin and other cryptocurrencies gained mainstream attention. The subsequent development of thousands of alternative cryptocurrencies, known as altcoins, has expanded the ecosystem, each offering unique features and use cases.

Cryptocurrencies are not merely digital currencies; they represent a broader shift towards decentralised systems. They enable peer-to-peer transactions, reduce transaction costs, and increase financial inclusivity, especially in regions with limited access to traditional banking services. Cryptocurrencies also facilitate the creation of decentralised applications (dApps) and smart contracts, which are self-executing contracts with the terms directly written into code. These innovations have the potential to revolutionise industries beyond finance, including supply chain management, healthcare, and real estate.

Understanding profit strategies in the cryptocurrency market is crucial due to the unique characteristics of these digital assets. Unlike traditional markets, cryptocurrencies are highly volatile, with prices capable of dramatic swings within short periods. This volatility presents both significant opportunities and risks for investors. Without a solid understanding of profit strategies, investors may find themselves vulnerable to market fluctuations, potentially leading to substantial financial losses.

By comprehending the various ways to profit from cryptocurrencies, such as long-term holding, trading, staking, and yield farming, investors can make informed decisions that align with their financial goals and risk tolerance. Each strategy comes with its own set of advantages and challenges, and a well-rounded knowledge base allows investors to diversify their approaches, thereby mitigating risks and enhancing potential returns.

Moreover, the cryptocurrency market operates 24/7, unlike traditional financial markets. This continuous operation requires investors to be more vigilant and responsive to market changes. Effective profit strategies often involve staying updated with the latest news, technological advancements, and regulatory developments that can impact market conditions.

Chapter 1: Understanding Cryptocurrency Basics

―――

What is Cryptocurrency?

Cryptocurrency, at its core, is a form of digital or virtual currency that uses cryptography for security. Unlike traditional currencies issued by governments (such as the pound or dollar), cryptocurrencies operate on technology known as blockchain, which ensures decentralisation, transparency, and immutability. This section will provide a clear definition of cryptocurrency and explain the key concepts underpinning this innovative technology.

Definition of Cryptocurrency

Cryptocurrency is a digital asset designed to work as a medium of exchange wherein individual coin ownership records are stored in a digital ledger using strong cryptographic algorithms. These cryptographic techniques secure transactions, control the creation of new units, and verify the transfer of assets. The decentralisation feature means that cryptocurrencies operate independently of a central bank or a single administrator.

Key Concepts

Blockchain Technology

At the heart of cryptocurrencies lies blockchain technology. A blockchain is a decentralised ledger that records all transactions across a network of computers. Each block in the chain contains several transactions, and every time a new transaction occurs, it is added to the existing chain. This chain of blocks is linked and secured using cryptographic hashes, making it extremely difficult to alter any individual block without changing all subsequent blocks, thus ensuring data integrity.

Decentralisation

One of the defining features of cryptocurrencies is decentralisation. Traditional financial systems rely on centralised authorities such as banks and governments to issue and regulate currency. In contrast, cryptocurrencies are typically decentralised and operate on a peer-to-peer network. This means that transactions occur directly between users without the need for intermediaries, reducing transaction costs and increasing the speed of transactions.

Cryptography

Cryptography is essential for the security and integrity of cryptocurrencies. It involves complex mathematical algorithms that secure data and ensure that transactions are conducted safely. Two main types of cryptographic techniques used in cryptocurrencies are public-key cryptography and hashing. Public-key cryptography involves a pair of keys (a public key and a private key) that enable users to receive and send cryptocurrency securely. Hashing ensures that the data within the blockchain remains unchanged and is verified with each transaction.

Consensus Mechanisms

Cryptocurrencies rely on consensus mechanisms to validate transactions and maintain the blockchain. The most common consensus mechanism is Proof of Work (PoW), used by Bitcoin, where miners solve complex mathematical problems to validate transactions and add new blocks to the blockchain. Another popular mechanism is Proof of Stake (PoS), where validators are chosen to create new blocks based on the number of coins they hold and are willing to 'stake' as collateral.

Wallets and Keys

Cryptocurrency wallets are digital tools that allow users to store, send, and receive digital assets. There are various types of wallets, including hardware wallets, software wallets, and paper wallets. Each wallet contains a public key, which acts as an address for receiving funds, and a private key, which is used to sign transactions and access the wallet's funds. Keeping the private key secure is crucial, as anyone with access to it can control the associated cryptocurrency.

Tokens and Coins

In the cryptocurrency world, the terms 'tokens' and 'coins' are often used interchangeably, but they have distinct meanings. Coins, like Bitcoin (BTC) and Ethereum (ETH), operate on their own blockchain and are typically used as a form of currency. Tokens, on the other hand, are created on existing blockchains (such as Ethereum's ERC-20 tokens) and can represent various assets or be used in decentralised applications (dApps).

Smart Contracts

Smart contracts are self-executing contracts with the terms of the agreement directly written into code. They automatically enforce and execute the terms of a contract when predefined conditions are met. Smart contracts run on blockchain platforms like Ethereum, enabling a wide range of applications, from financial services to supply chain management, without the need for intermediaries.

Understanding these key concepts is essential for anyone looking to delve into the world of cryptocurrencies. They form the foundation upon which various profit strategies are built, and grasping these basics will enable you to navigate the more complex aspects of cryptocurrency investment and trading effectively. In the following chapters, we will explore how these concepts are applied in real-world scenarios and how you can leverage them to maximise your crypto profits.

How Blockchain Technology Works

An Overview of Blockchain

Blockchain technology is the backbone of cryptocurrency, providing the structure that enables decentralised digital transactions. At its simplest, a blockchain is a digital ledger composed of records called blocks, which are securely linked together in a chain using cryptographic principles. Each block contains a list of transactions and a reference to the previous block, creating a continuous and unalterable chain of records.

When a transaction is initiated, it is broadcast to a network of computers, known as nodes. These nodes validate the transaction using a consensus mechanism, ensuring that all transactions are legitimate and preventing double-spending. Once validated, the transaction is grouped with others into a block. This block is then added to the blockchain, becoming a permanent part of the ledger. Every node in the network maintains a copy of the blockchain, ensuring that all participants have the same information and contributing to the transparency and security of the system.

One of the most innovative aspects of blockchain technology is its decentralisation. Unlike traditional ledgers, which are typically managed by a single central authority, a blockchain operates on a distributed network of nodes. This decentralisation removes the need for intermediaries, reduces the risk of single points of failure, and enhances the security and integrity of the data.

Security and Decentralisation

Security

The security of blockchain technology is multi-faceted, relying on cryptographic techniques and a distributed consensus mechanism. Each block in the blockchain contains a cryptographic hash of the previous block, a timestamp, and transaction data. The hash function transforms the block's information into a fixed-size string of characters, creating a unique fingerprint for each block. Any attempt to alter the data in a block would change its hash, making the tampering immediately detectable.

Moreover, before a block is added to the blockchain, it must be validated by the network nodes through a consensus mechanism. In the Proof of Work (PoW) consensus, for example, miners compete to solve a complex mathematical problem. The first miner to solve the problem gets to add the block to the blockchain and is rewarded with cryptocurrency. This process requires significant computational power, making it impractical for malicious actors to alter the blockchain as they would need to control a majority of the network's computing power.

Another consensus mechanism is Proof of Stake (PoS), where validators are chosen to create new blocks based on the number of coins they hold and are willing to "stake" as collateral. This method is energy-efficient compared to PoW and also ensures that validators have a vested interest in maintaining the network's integrity, as any malicious behaviour could result in the loss of their staked coins.

Decentralisation

Decentralisation is a cornerstone of blockchain technology, providing numerous advantages over centralised systems. In a decentralised network, no single entity has control over the entire blockchain. Instead, control is distributed among all participating nodes, making the system more resilient to attacks and failures. If one node goes offline or is compromised, the network continues to function seamlessly, as other nodes maintain the blockchain.

This distribution of control also enhances trust and transparency. All transactions are recorded on a public ledger, which is accessible to all network participants. This transparency ensures that all parties can verify transactions independently, reducing the need for trust in a central authority. Furthermore, because the blockchain is immutable, once a block is added, it cannot be altered without altering all subsequent blocks, which would require the consensus of the majority of the network. This immutability ensures that the data recorded on the blockchain is accurate and tamper-proof.

Decentralisation also promotes inclusivity and accessibility. Traditional financial systems often exclude individuals who lack access to banking infrastructure. In contrast, blockchain technology allows anyone with an internet connection to participate in the network, enabling peer-to-peer transactions across the globe without the need for intermediaries.

Types of Cryptocurrencies

The cryptocurrency market is vast and diverse, encompassing a wide range of digital assets with varying purposes and functionalities. At the forefront is Bitcoin, the first and most well-known cryptocurrency, often referred to as digital gold due to its store of value properties and deflationary nature. Bitcoin's primary use case is as a decentralised digital currency, enabling peer-to-peer transactions without the need for a central authority.

Following Bitcoin, numerous alternative cryptocurrencies, or altcoins have been developed, each aiming to improve upon Bitcoin's limitations or serve unique use cases. Ethereum, for instance, introduced the concept of smart contracts, which are self-executing contracts with the terms of the agreement directly written into code. This innovation has enabled the creation of decentralised applications (dApps) and has spawned a whole ecosystem of tokens built on the Ethereum blockchain, known as ERC-20 tokens. These tokens can represent anything from digital assets to voting rights in a decentralised organisation.

Other notable cryptocurrencies include Ripple (XRP), which focuses on fast and low-cost international money transfers. Ripple's technology is designed to enable real-time, cross-border payment systems that are more efficient than traditional banking systems. Similarly, Litecoin (LTC) aims to provide quicker transaction confirmations compared to Bitcoin, with a focus on becoming a global payment system.

Privacy-focused coins like Monero (XMR) and Zcash (ZEC) offer enhanced anonymity features, appealing to users who prioritise privacy. Monero uses advanced cryptographic techniques to obscure transaction details, ensuring that senders, recipients, and transaction amounts remain private. Zcash offers the option of "shielded" transactions, which encrypt transaction data on the blockchain.

Stablecoins, such as Tether (USDT) and USD Coin (USDC), are pegged to fiat currencies, providing a stable value that mitigates the volatility typically associated with cryptocurrencies. These coins are often used for trading, as a store of value, or as a means of transferring value between exchanges without exposure to price fluctuations.

Additionally, there are cryptocurrencies designed for specific industries or purposes. For example, Chainlink (LINK) provides decentralised oracle services that enable smart contracts to securely interact with real-world data. Binance Coin (BNB), originally created as a utility token for the Binance cryptocurrency exchange, offers various benefits to users such as reduced trading fees.

DeFi (Decentralised Finance) tokens, like Uniswap (UNI) and Aave (AAVE), power platforms that aim to replicate traditional financial services such as lending, borrowing, and trading, but in a decentralised manner without intermediaries. These tokens often provide governance rights, allowing holders to vote on key decisions affecting the protocol.

This diversity allows investors to choose from a wide array of options tailored to different needs, risk appetites, and investment strategies, making the cryptocurrency market a rich landscape for exploration and profit. Whether you are looking to invest in a stable, low-risk asset, or a high-potential, high-risk venture, the variety of cryptocurrencies available offers numerous opportunities to diversify and optimise your investment portfolio.

Risks and Rewards

Investing in cryptocurrencies presents a compelling yet complex landscape of risk and reward, predominantly shaped by the market's inherent volatility. Cryptocurrencies are notoriously volatile, with values capable of experiencing significant surges or steep declines within very short time frames. This volatility stems from various factors, including market sentiment, technological advancements, regulatory changes, and macroeconomic conditions. For instance, a single announcement from a prominent figure or institution can send prices soaring, while news of regulatory crackdowns or security breaches can trigger sharp declines.

Understanding and capitalising on market trends is essential for navigating this volatility effectively. Investors need to stay informed about current events and trends that can impact the market. This includes monitoring technological developments, such as updates to blockchain protocols, and assessing their potential to drive adoption and increase asset values. Regulatory news, both positive and negative, can also significantly influence market dynamics. For example, favourable regulations in major economies can boost investor confidence and drive prices up, while restrictive policies can have the opposite effect.

The potential for profit in the cryptocurrency market is substantial, particularly for those who can adeptly navigate its fluctuations. Early adopters of successful projects often see exponential returns on their investments. Bitcoin's rise from a few cents to tens of thousands of dollars is a prime example of the massive profit potential. Altcoins, while generally more volatile, also present opportunities for significant gains. Ethereum's smart contracts have revolutionised the industry, leading to substantial increases in its value and the values of related tokens.

To manage the risks associated with this volatility, investors employ various strategies. Diversification is a fundamental approach, spreading investments across different assets to mitigate the impact of any single asset's poor performance. Additionally, setting stop-loss orders can help limit losses by automatically selling an asset when its price falls to a predetermined level. Technical analysis, which involves studying price charts and market indicators, can also provide valuable insights into potential market movements, helping investors make more informed decisions.

Staking and yield farming offer ways to earn passive income, albeit with their own risks. Staking involves holding certain cryptocurrencies in a wallet to support network operations, earning rewards in return. Yield farming, part of the decentralised finance (DeFi) movement, involves providing liquidity to DeFi platforms in exchange for interest or additional tokens. While these strategies can generate steady returns, they also expose investors to risks like token devaluation and smart contract vulnerabilities.

Despite these risks, the allure of substantial profits continues to attract investors to the cryptocurrency market. The key to success lies in balancing the high potential rewards with a disciplined approach to managing risk. This includes staying informed, employing sound investment strategies, and being prepared to adapt to the rapidly evolving market landscape. By doing so, investors can position themselves to take advantage of the opportunities presented by this exciting and dynamic market, while also protecting their investments from its inherent uncertainties.

Chapter 2: Buy and Hold (HODL)

Description

The "Buy and Hold" strategy, often referred to in the cryptocurrency community as "HODL" (a term that originated from a misspelled forum post meaning "hold"), is a long-term investment strategy. This approach involves purchasing a cryptocurrency and holding onto it for an extended period, regardless of market fluctuations. The underlying principle of HODL is the belief in the long-term potential of the cryptocurrency, expecting that its value will increase significantly over time. Unlike active trading, which requires frequent buying and selling based on short-term price movements, HODLing focuses on weathering market volatility with the aim of capitalising on the overall upward trend.

Investors who adopt the HODL strategy typically choose cryptocurrencies they believe will grow due to their technological innovation, market adoption, or strong fundamentals. Bitcoin, Ethereum, and other major cryptocurrencies are common choices for HODLers because of their established market positions and ongoing development efforts. This strategy is rooted in the belief that the cryptocurrency market, despite its inherent volatility, will continue to grow as digital currencies gain broader acceptance and integration into the global financial system.

Advantages

One of the primary advantages of the HODL strategy is its simplicity and minimal time investment. Unlike day trading or swing trading, which require constant monitoring of market conditions and timely decision-making, HODLing is relatively passive. Once an investment decision is made, the investor can hold onto their assets without the need for frequent intervention. This makes it an ideal strategy for individuals who may not have the time or inclination to engage in active trading.

Another significant advantage of HODLing is the potential for substantial long-term gains. Historical data has shown that, despite periods of significant volatility, the value of leading cryptocurrencies like Bitcoin and Ethereum has generally trended upward over time. Early adopters who invested in Bitcoin, for example, have seen astronomical returns on their investments. By holding onto their assets through market ups and downs, HODLers position themselves to benefit from the overall growth trajectory of the cryptocurrency market.

Additionally, the HODL strategy can reduce the psychological stress associated with frequent trading. Active trading requires making numerous decisions, often under pressure, which can lead to anxiety and emotional decision-making. In contrast, HODLing involves a long-term commitment and a more hands-off approach, allowing investors to avoid the stress of short-term market fluctuations and focus on the potential long-term rewards.

Risks

While the HODL strategy offers several advantages, it is not without risks. One of the most significant risks is market volatility. Cryptocurrencies are known for their price fluctuations, and substantial declines can occur within short periods. Investors need to be prepared for the possibility that their holdings may lose value, sometimes dramatically, during market downturns. The psychological resilience required to maintain a HODLing position during such times cannot be underestimated.

Another risk associated with the HODL strategy is the patience required. Unlike short-term trading strategies that can provide quicker returns, HODLing is a long-term commitment. It may take years for an investment to realise its full potential, and there are no guarantees of future performance. Investors must be willing to lock up their capital for extended periods, potentially missing out on other investment opportunities.

Furthermore, the cryptocurrency market is still relatively young and evolving. Regulatory changes, technological advancements, and market dynamics can all impact the future value of cryptocurrencies. For example, increased regulatory scrutiny or adverse legal decisions could negatively affect the market, while technological breakthroughs by competitors could erode the market position of a given cryptocurrency. HODLers must remain vigilant and informed about such developments to mitigate these risks.

Case Studies

One of the most compelling and illustrative examples of the HODL strategy's success is the case of Bitcoin investor Kristoffer Koch. In 2009, Koch, a Norwegian engineer, stumbled upon Bitcoin while writing a thesis on encryption. Intrigued by the concept of a decentralised digital currency, he decided to invest a modest amount of money—150 Norwegian kroner (approximately $27 at that time)—to purchase 5,000 Bitcoins.

At the time of his purchase, Bitcoin was still in its infancy, and its value was almost negligible. For several years, Koch paid little attention to his investment, considering it more of an academic curiosity than a serious financial venture. During this period, Bitcoin experienced significant volatility, with its price fluctuating wildly and facing scepticism and uncertainty from the broader financial community.

In 2013, four years after his initial investment, Koch's curiosity was piqued when he started hearing more about Bitcoin's growing prominence. He decided to check on his long-forgotten investment. To his astonishment, the 5,000 Bitcoins he had purchased for $27 were now worth approximately $886,000. Bitcoin's price had skyrocketed from fractions of a cent to over $200 per coin.

Koch's decision to HODL—whether intentional or due to his initial neglect—had paid off extraordinarily well. He cashed out a portion of his Bitcoins, using the proceeds to purchase an apartment in one of Oslo's most affluent neighbourhoods. Despite the subsequent market corrections and volatility, the value of Bitcoin continued to rise over the years, validating Koch's long-term approach.

Koch's case underscores several key aspects of the HODL strategy. Firstly, it highlights the potential for significant long-term gains. By holding onto his Bitcoins through periods of market uncertainty and volatility, Koch was able to benefit from the overall upward trajectory of Bitcoin's value. His initial investment, which many would have considered risky and speculative, turned into a life-changing sum due to the appreciation of Bitcoin over time.

Secondly, this case study illustrates the psychological resilience required for successful HODLing. During the early years, Bitcoin's value was highly volatile, and it faced numerous regulatory and technical challenges. Many early adopters might have been tempted to sell during periods of sharp declines, fearing a complete loss of their investment. However, those who maintained their conviction in Bitcoin's long-term potential and held on to their assets were ultimately rewarded.

Lastly, Koch's experience highlights the importance of staying informed. Although he initially forgot about his investment, his eventual awareness of Bitcoin's increasing value prompted him to revisit and realise his gains. Continuous engagement with the market, even if it's just periodic check-ins, can help investors make timely decisions regarding their holdings.

In conclusion, Kristoffer Koch's Bitcoin investment is a prime example of the potential rewards associated with the HODL strategy. By purchasing and holding Bitcoin for several years, Koch turned a modest investment into a substantial fortune. His story serves as an inspiration for long-term investors, demonstrating that, despite the inherent risks and volatility of the cryptocurrency market, patient and informed HODLing can lead to significant financial rewards.

Chapter 3: Trading Strategies

Trading cryptocurrencies can be highly rewarding but also fraught with significant risks due to the market's inherent volatility. This chapter explores three popular trading strategies: Day Trading, Swing Trading, and Technical Analysis. Each strategy offers unique advantages and requires specific skills and tools to be executed successfully.

1. Day Trading

Day trading involves buying and selling cryptocurrencies within a single trading day. The goal is to profit from short-term price movements. Day traders make multiple trades throughout the day, closing all positions before the market closes to avoid overnight risks. This strategy demands a high level of attention and quick decision-making as traders capitalise on small price fluctuations.

Advantages

The primary advantage of day trading is the potential for high profits within a short period. By taking advantage of intraday price movements, traders can accumulate gains rapidly. Because positions are closed before the end of the day, day traders avoid the risks associated with overnight price changes and market gaps that can occur when trading resumes. Additionally, day trading allows for a significant amount of trading activity, providing more opportunities to profit from the market's volatility.

Risks

Day trading is highly risky and can lead to significant losses if not managed properly. The rapid pace of trading requires constant monitoring of the markets and quick decision-making, which can be stressful and lead to emotional trading. High-frequency trading also incurs higher transaction fees, which can eat into profits. Moreover, the volatile nature of cryptocurrencies means that sudden and unexpected market movements can result in substantial losses. Another risk is the potential for burnout due to the intense focus and time commitment required.

Tips and Tools for Success

1. **Develop a Trading Plan**: A well-defined trading plan includes entry and exit points, risk management strategies, and criteria for selecting trades. Stick to this plan to avoid impulsive decisions.
2. **Use Stop-Loss Orders**: Protect your investments by setting stop-loss orders to automatically sell assets if their price drops to a predetermined level.
3. **Stay Informed**: Keep up with market news, events, and trends that could impact cryptocurrency prices. Use reliable news sources and trading platforms with real-time data.
4. **Technical Analysis Tools**: Utilize technical analysis tools such as candlestick charts, moving averages, and volume indicators to identify trading opportunities.
5. **Trading Bots**: Consider using automated trading bots that execute trades based on predefined criteria, helping to reduce emotional decision-making and increase efficiency.
6. **Practice with Paper Trading**: Use demo accounts to practice trading without risking real money. This can help you refine your strategies and build confidence.

1. **Swing Trading**

Swing trading involves holding onto a cryptocurrency for several days to weeks to profit from expected price swings. Unlike day trading, which focuses on minute-to-minute price changes, swing trading aims to capture larger price movements over a longer period. This strategy requires a thorough understanding of market cycles and trends. Swing traders look for opportunities where they believe the price of a cryptocurrency will move significantly in a particular direction within a short to medium timeframe.

Advantages

Swing trading offers a balance between the high-frequency, high-risk nature of day trading and the long-term commitment of HODLing. It allows traders to take advantage of market volatility without the need for constant monitoring. By focusing on medium-term trends, swing traders can achieve substantial profits with fewer trades compared to day trading. This strategy also provides more flexibility, allowing traders to continue with other activities without needing to be glued to the screen all day.

Risks

While less hectic than day trading, swing trading still carries significant risks. Market trends can reverse unexpectedly, leading to potential losses. Holding positions for longer periods also exposes traders to overnight and weekend market risks. Additionally, swing traders need to be proficient in technical and fundamental analysis to accurately predict market movements. There is also the risk of holding onto a position for too long, missing the optimal point to take profits or cut losses.

Market Analysis Techniques

    a. **Trend Analysis**: Identify the overall direction of the market (uptrend, downtrend, or sideways) using tools like trend lines and moving averages. Trading in the direction of the trend increases the probability of success.

b. **Support and Resistance Levels**: Determine key price levels where the asset tends to find support (bottom) and resistance (top). These levels can signal potential entry and exit points for trades.

c. **Technical Indicators**: Use indicators such as the Relative Strength Index (RSI), Moving Average Convergence Divergence (MACD), and Bollinger Bands to identify overbought or oversold conditions and potential price reversals.

d. **Chart Patterns**: Recognize chart patterns like head and shoulders, double tops/bottoms, and triangles to predict future price movements.

e. **Fundamental Analysis**: Consider broader market conditions, news, and events that could influence the price of the cryptocurrency. Combining fundamental insights with technical analysis can enhance the accuracy of predictions.

f. **Volume Analysis**: Assess trading volume to confirm trends. Increasing volume during an uptrend can indicate a strong bullish trend, while decreasing volume may signal a potential reversal.

Technical Analysis - Using Charts and Data

Technical analysis is the study of historical price and volume data to forecast future price movements. It relies on charts and various analytical tools to identify patterns and trends that can inform trading decisions. Unlike fundamental analysis, which evaluates the intrinsic value of an asset, technical analysis focuses purely on market data. By analysing past price movements and trading volumes, traders can predict future behaviour and identify trading opportunities.

Key Indicators and Patterns

I. **Candlestick Charts**: Candlestick charts provide a visual representation of price movements over a specific period. Each candlestick shows the opening, closing, high, and low prices, offering insights into market sentiment and potential reversals. Patterns like Doji, Hammer, and Engulfing can indicate market turning points.

II. **Moving Averages**: Moving averages smooth out price data to identify trends. The Simple Moving Average (SMA) and Exponential Moving Average (EMA) are commonly used to determine the direction of the trend and potential support and resistance levels. Crossovers between short-term and long-term moving averages can signal buy or sell opportunities.

III. **Relative Strength Index (RSI)**: RSI measures the speed and change of price movements, indicating overbought or oversold conditions. An RSI above 70 suggests overbought conditions, while an RSI below 30 indicates oversold conditions. Divergences between RSI and price can signal potential reversals.

IV. **Moving Average Convergence Divergence (MACD)**: MACD is a trend-following momentum indicator that shows the relationship between two moving averages. It helps identify bullish or bearish momentum and potential buy or sell signals. The MACD line crossing above the signal line can be a bullish signal, while crossing below can be bearish.

V. **Bollinger Bands**: Bollinger Bands consist of a middle band (SMA) and two outer bands representing standard deviations from the mean. They help identify volatility and potential overbought or oversold conditions. When the price touches the upper band, it may be overbought; when it touches the lower band, it may be oversold.

VI. **Support and Resistance Levels**: Identifying these levels helps traders understand where the price is likely to encounter obstacles. Breakouts above resistance or breakdowns below support can signal strong buy or sell opportunities. These levels can also serve as stop-loss or take-profit points.

VII. **Chart Patterns**: Patterns like head and shoulders, double tops/bottoms, and triangles provide visual cues about future price movements. Recognising these patterns can help predict potential price breakouts or reversals. For example, a head and shoulders pattern typically signals a bearish reversal, while a double bottom indicates a bullish reversal.

By mastering these trading strategies and analytical techniques, traders can enhance their ability to make informed decisions and potentially profit from the dynamic cryptocurrency market. Whether you prefer the rapid pace of day trading, the more measured approach of swing trading, or the detailed analysis provided by technical analysis, understanding these methods is crucial for successful trading. Staying disciplined, informed, and adaptable will help you navigate the complexities of the cryptocurrency market and maximise your potential for profit.

Chapter 4: Staking

Crypto staking is a process that involves participating in the validation of transactions on a blockchain network through the holding and locking up of a specific amount of cryptocurrency. Unlike Proof of Work (PoW) systems, which rely on miners solving complex mathematical problems to validate transactions and secure the network, staking operates on a Proof of Stake (PoS) consensus mechanism. In a PoS system, the right to validate transactions and create new blocks is determined by the amount of cryptocurrency a participant holds and is willing to "stake" as collateral. Essentially, staking involves committing your cryptocurrency to support the operations of a blockchain network in return for rewards.

When you stake your cryptocurrency, you are essentially locking up your funds in a wallet for a set period. These staked funds contribute to the network's security and efficiency, as they are used to validate transactions and produce new blocks. The more cryptocurrency you stake, the higher your chances of being selected to validate a block and earn rewards. These rewards typically come in the form of additional cryptocurrency, akin to earning interest on a savings account. The rewards are distributed proportionally, meaning the more you stake, the more you can potentially earn.

Staking can be done individually or through staking pools. Individual staking requires a certain level of technical expertise and resources, as you need to run a node and maintain it continuously to stay online and eligible for rewards. On the other hand, staking pools allow multiple participants to combine their resources and increase their chances of validating transactions and earning rewards. Participants in a staking pool share the rewards proportionally to their contributions.

One of the significant advantages of staking is that it provides a way to earn passive income from your cryptocurrency holdings without the need for extensive hardware or energy consumption, unlike mining. Additionally, staking helps support the network's stability and security, making it more robust against attacks. However, there are also risks involved, such as the potential for the staked cryptocurrency to lose value over time, or penalties for malicious behaviour or prolonged downtime in some staking protocols.

Passive Income Generation

One of the most compelling advantages of crypto staking is the ability to generate passive income. When you stake your cryptocurrency, you earn rewards simply by holding and securing the network, like earning interest in a traditional savings account. This income can be especially attractive in the context of low-yield traditional financial products. The rates of return on staking can be significantly higher than those offered by savings accounts or bonds, making it a lucrative option for those willing to invest in cryptocurrencies. The process of earning through staking is relatively hands-off, allowing you to generate income without the need for active trading or constant monitoring of market movements. This can be particularly appealing to investors who prefer a more passive approach to growing their wealth.

Compound Growth

Staking also offers the potential for compound growth. By reinvesting the rewards, you earn back into your staking portfolio, you can increase your staked amount and, consequently, your future rewards. This compounding effect can significantly boost your overall returns over time. The longer you stake and reinvest, the more substantial your rewards can become, leveraging the power of compound interest in the context of cryptocurrency investments.

Network Security and Stability

Beyond the financial incentives, staking plays a crucial role in supporting the security and stability of blockchain networks. In a Proof of Stake (PoS) system, validators are selected to create new blocks and validate transactions based on the amount of cryptocurrency they hold and stake. By participating in staking, you are helping to decentralise and secure the network. A well-distributed and robust staking base reduces the risk of centralisation, where a few entities control the majority of the network's validating power. This decentralisation is fundamental to the integrity and resilience of the blockchain, as it makes the network more resistant to attacks and manipulations.

Environmental Efficiency

Staking is also environmentally friendlier compared to the energy-intensive process of mining, which is used in Proof of Work (PoW) systems. Mining requires vast amounts of computational power and electricity, which has raised concerns about its environmental impact. In contrast, staking relies on existing cryptocurrency holdings to secure the network, resulting in a much lower carbon footprint. By choosing to stake rather than mine, participants can support the sustainability of blockchain technology while still earning rewards.

Community Engagement and Governance

Staking often comes with additional benefits, such as the ability to participate in the governance of the blockchain network. Many PoS-based cryptocurrencies grant stakers voting rights on important network decisions, such as protocol upgrades, changes to reward structures, or other critical developments. This governance model fosters a more engaged and active community, as stakeholders have a direct say in the future direction of the network. By staking, you are not only earning rewards but also contributing to the democratic process that helps shape the blockchain ecosystem.

Reduced Market Volatility Impact

Finally, staking can help mitigate the impact of market volatility on your investment portfolio. By committing to stake your cryptocurrency for a specific period, you are less likely to make impulsive decisions based on short-term price movements. This disciplined approach can help you stay focused on long-term growth and reduce the emotional stress associated with market fluctuations. Moreover, the steady stream of rewards can provide a buffer against market downturns, offering a source of income even during periods of price decline.

Risks

Coin Value Fluctuation

One of the most significant risks associated with staking is the potential for coin value fluctuation. Cryptocurrencies are known for their high volatility, and the value of the staked coins can experience dramatic changes over short periods. If the market value of the staked cryptocurrency declines significantly during the staking period, the fiat value of the rewards earned, and the staked principal can be adversely affected. For instance, even if you earn a high percentage of staking rewards, a substantial drop in the coin's market value can negate these gains, resulting in a net loss.

Lock-Up Periods

Many staking protocols require a lock-up period during which the staked coins cannot be withdrawn or sold. This period can range from a few days to several months, depending on the network. While your coins are locked up, you are unable to liquidate them in response to market movements. If the value of the cryptocurrency drops significantly during this lock-up period, you could face considerable losses without the ability to mitigate them by selling your holdings.

Liquidity Risks

Staking also involves liquidity risks. The lock-up period restricts your ability to access your funds quickly. In a rapidly changing market, the inability to access your staked coins can be a disadvantage, especially if you need liquidity to respond to market opportunities or emergencies. Additionally, some staking platforms may take several days to release your funds even after the lock-up period ends, further delaying your access to liquidity.

Network Risks

The security and stability of the blockchain network itself pose another risk. While Proof of Stake (PoS) networks are generally considered secure, they are not immune to attacks or technical failures. Network vulnerabilities, such as bugs in the staking protocol or smart contract flaws, can potentially lead to loss of staked funds. For example, if a network experiences a 51% attack, where a single entity gains control of most of the staking power, it can manipulate transactions and potentially compromise the integrity of the entire network.

Slashing Risks

In PoS networks, validators are expected to act in the network's best interest. However, if a validator behaves maliciously or negligently—such as by double-signing transactions or experiencing prolonged downtime—they may face penalties known as "slashing." Slashing results in the loss of a portion or all of the staked funds as a penalty for misbehavior. If you are participating in a staking pool, the actions of the pool operator can affect your staked funds, even if you personally did nothing wrong.

Inflation Risks

While staking rewards can be lucrative, they often come from the issuance of new coins, leading to inflation. If the rate of new coin issuance outpaces the demand for the cryptocurrency, it can lead to inflation, reducing the value of both the staked coins and the rewards earned. This inflationary effect can erode the purchasing power of your holdings over time, potentially offsetting the gains from staking.

Opportunity Costs

Staking your cryptocurrency also involves opportunity costs. By locking up your funds in a staking contract, you might miss out on other investment opportunities that could offer higher returns. In a rapidly evolving market, the ability to quickly pivot and invest in new promising projects is crucial. The lock-up periods associated with staking can limit this flexibility and potential for higher gains elsewhere.

Regulatory Risks

The regulatory environment for cryptocurrencies is still developing and varies significantly across jurisdictions. Changes in regulations can impact the legality and profitability of staking activities. For example, new regulations could impose additional reporting requirements, taxes, or even outright bans on certain staking activities, which could negatively affect your staking returns and the usability of your staked funds.

Technical Risks

Staking requires a certain level of technical knowledge, especially if you are running your own staking node. Misconfigurations, software bugs, or security breaches can lead to the loss of staked funds. Even if you are using a staking pool or a third-party service, there is a risk that the platform could experience technical failures or be hacked, resulting in a loss of your funds.

Examples of Popular Staking Coins and Platforms

Popular Staking Coins

- **Ethereum 2.0 (ETH)**
    - **Overview**: Ethereum, the second-largest cryptocurrency by market capitalization, is transitioning from a Proof of Work (PoW) to a Proof of Stake (PoS) consensus mechanism through Ethereum 2.0. This upgrade aims to improve scalability, security, and energy efficiency.
    - **Staking Requirements**: A minimum of 32 ETH is required to become a validator and participate in staking directly. However, smaller holders can stake through various staking pools.
    - **Rewards**: Staking rewards can vary but are generally around 4-10% annually, depending on the total amount of ETH staked and network conditions.
- **Cardano (ADA)**
    - **Overview**: Cardano is a blockchain platform that aims to provide a secure and scalable infrastructure for decentralized applications. Its native cryptocurrency, ADA, is used for staking.
    - **Staking Requirements**: There is no minimum amount required to stake ADA, making it accessible to a wide range of investors. ADA can be staked directly through the Cardano wallet or via staking pools.
    - **Rewards**: Staking rewards typically range from

4-6% annually, with variations based on the performance of the staking pool and network conditions.

- **Polkadot (DOT)**
  - **Overview**: Polkadot is a multi-chain blockchain platform designed to facilitate interoperability between different blockchains. DOT is its native token used for staking and governance.
  - **Staking Requirements**: A minimum of 1 DOT is required to participate in staking, though higher amounts are often necessary to be selected as a validator. Many users opt for staking through pools.
  - **Rewards**: Staking rewards for DOT are generally between 10-15% annually, influenced by network participation and the amount of DOT staked.
- **Tezos (XTZ)**
  - **Overview**: Tezos is a self-amending blockchain platform that supports smart contracts and decentralized applications. XTZ, its native cryptocurrency, is used for staking, referred to as "baking."
  - **Staking Requirements**: A minimum of 8,000 XTZ is required to become a baker (validator). Smaller holders can delegate their XTZ to bakers through staking services.
  - **Rewards**: Annual rewards for staking Tezos typically range from 5-7%, depending on the network's inflation rate and the chosen baker's performance.
- **Cosmos (ATOM)**
  - **Overview**: Cosmos aims to create an internet of

blockchains, enabling different blockchains to communicate and interoperate. ATOM is its native staking token.

- **Staking Requirements**: There is no minimum requirement for staking ATOM, and users can stake through validators.
- **Rewards**: Staking rewards for ATOM usually range from 7-10% annually, with fluctuations based on network conditions and the number of tokens staked.

Popular Staking Platforms

- **Binance**
  - **Overview**: Binance is one of the largest cryptocurrency exchanges globally, offering a range of staking services for various cryptocurrencies.
  - **Features**: Users can stake multiple cryptocurrencies directly on the platform, including ETH, ADA, DOT, XTZ, and more. Binance provides flexible and locked staking options, with varying durations and reward rates.
  - **Rewards**: Rewards vary based on the staked cryptocurrency and the chosen staking option, often offering competitive rates compared to other platforms.
- **Kraken**
  - **Overview**: Kraken is a reputable cryptocurrency exchange that offers staking services for several popular cryptocurrencies.
  - **Features**: Kraken supports staking for coins like

ETH, ADA, DOT, and XTZ, among others. The platform provides detailed information on staking rewards and allows users to unstake their assets at any time.

- **Rewards**: Staking rewards on Kraken are competitive, with rates generally ranging from 4-12% annually, depending on the cryptocurrency.

- **Coinbase**
  - **Overview**: Coinbase is a widely used cryptocurrency exchange, particularly popular in the United States, that offers staking services.
  - **Features**: Users can stake a select number of cryptocurrencies, including ETH and ADA, directly through the platform. Coinbase simplifies the staking process, making it accessible to beginners.
  - **Rewards**: Rewards on Coinbase vary by cryptocurrency but are typically in the range of 4-7% annually.

- **Staked**
  - **Overview**: Staked is a platform dedicated to providing staking and lending services for institutional and individual investors.
  - **Features**: Staked supports a wide range of PoS cryptocurrencies, including ETH, ADA, DOT, XTZ, and ATOM. The platform offers non-custodial staking solutions, ensuring that users retain control of their assets.
  - **Rewards**: Rewards on Staked are competitive and vary by cryptocurrency, often ranging from 5-15% annually.

- **Ledger Live**

- **Overview**: Ledger Live is a software application that works with Ledger hardware wallets, providing a secure way to manage and stake cryptocurrencies.
- **Features**: Users can stake several cryptocurrencies, including XTZ, ATOM, and DOT, directly from their Ledger hardware wallets. This ensures high security while earning staking rewards.
- **Rewards**: Staking rewards on Ledger Live vary by cryptocurrency but are generally competitive, offering rates similar to those found on major exchanges.

In conclusion, staking presents a promising way to earn passive income while supporting the security and operations of blockchain networks. By choosing popular staking coins like Ethereum 2.0, Cardano, Polkadot, Tezos, and Cosmos, and utilizing reliable platforms such as Binance, Kraken, Coinbase, Staked, and Ledger Live, investors can effectively participate in staking with varying degrees of flexibility, security, and potential rewards.

Chapter 5: Yield Farming and Liquidity Mining

Yield farming and liquidity mining are advanced investment strategies within the decentralized finance (DeFi) ecosystem that involve providing liquidity to DeFi protocols in exchange for rewards. These strategies have gained significant popularity due to their potential for high returns, although they come with substantial risks. Understanding how they work and the intricacies involved is crucial for anyone looking to venture into this aspect of the cryptocurrency world.

Providing Liquidity to DeFi Protocols

At the core of yield farming and liquidity mining is the concept of providing liquidity to DeFi protocols. DeFi protocols are decentralized applications (dApps) built on blockchain networks, primarily Ethereum, that offer financial services such as lending, borrowing, trading, and earning interest without intermediaries like banks. To function effectively, these protocols require liquidity, which is the availability of assets to facilitate transactions.

Liquidity providers (LPs) supply assets to a liquidity pool, a smart contract that holds funds and enables decentralized trading, lending, or borrowing. In return for providing liquidity, LPs receive rewards, often in the form of additional tokens. These rewards can come from transaction fees generated by the protocol, interest from loans, or newly issued tokens designed to incentivize participation.

Yield farming typically involves moving assets across various DeFi protocols to maximize returns. Farmers strategically allocate their funds to different pools, aiming to earn the highest yield possible.

Liquidity mining is a subset of yield farming where participants receive tokens as rewards for providing liquidity, often involving new or less established DeFi projects that use this mechanism to bootstrap liquidity and attract users.

Advantages

High Returns

One of the primary advantages of yield farming and liquidity mining is the potential for high returns. The DeFi space offers much higher yields compared to traditional financial instruments. In some cases, annual percentage yields (APYs) can reach triple digits, particularly for new projects looking to attract liquidity quickly. These high returns are made possible by the competitive nature of DeFi protocols and the innovative incentive structures they employ.

Rewards from yield farming are typically paid out in the native tokens of the platform or other cryptocurrencies. These tokens can often be reinvested into other liquidity pools or sold on the open market for profit. The compounding effect of reinvesting earned tokens can significantly amplify returns over time. Moreover, participating in liquidity mining can sometimes grant access to new tokens at an early stage, which might appreciate in value if the project succeeds.

Yield farming also allows for flexibility and active management of funds. Investors can move their assets between different protocols and pools to take advantage of the best opportunities. This dynamic approach enables yield farmers to maximize their earnings by adapting to changing market conditions and shifting liquidity demands.

Risks

Smart Contract Vulnerabilities

Despite the allure of high returns, yield farming and liquidity mining come with substantial risks. One of the most significant risks is smart contract vulnerabilities. DeFi protocols are built on smart contracts—self-executing contracts with the terms of the agreement directly written into code. While smart contracts aim to eliminate the need for intermediaries and provide transparency, they are not immune to bugs or security flaws.

If a smart contract contains a vulnerability, it can be exploited by malicious actors, potentially leading to significant financial losses for liquidity providers. High-profile hacks and exploits in the DeFi space have resulted in millions of dollars in losses, highlighting the importance of conducting thorough due diligence before investing. Audits by reputable firms can provide some assurance, but they do not guarantee absolute security.

Impermanent Loss

Another critical risk associated with yield farming is impermanent loss. Impermanent loss occurs when the price of the assets provided to a liquidity pool changes relative to their price at the time of deposit. When liquidity providers supply assets to a pool, they receive liquidity provider (LP) tokens representing their share of the pool. As the prices of the underlying assets fluctuate, the value of these LP tokens can diverge from the value of holding the assets directly.

If the price of one asset in the pool increases significantly compared to the other, the LP may end up with a smaller amount of the higher-performing asset when they withdraw their funds. This loss is termed "impermanent" because it only materializes when the assets are withdrawn from the pool. If the price ratio returns to the initial state, the impermanent loss can diminish. However, in volatile markets, impermanent loss can significantly impact the profitability of yield farming.

Regulatory Risks

Regulatory uncertainty is another risk factor. The legal landscape for DeFi is still evolving, and regulatory actions could impact the operation and profitability of DeFi protocols. Governments and regulatory bodies are scrutinizing the DeFi space for potential compliance issues, such as money laundering and unregistered securities offerings. Changes in regulations could impose new requirements on DeFi projects, potentially affecting liquidity and returns.

Market Volatility

Market volatility also poses a risk to yield farming. Cryptocurrency prices are notoriously volatile, and sudden market movements can affect the value of staked assets and earned rewards. In a bear market, the value of both the staked assets and the rewards can decrease significantly, leading to reduced returns or losses.

Popular Platforms - Examples and Strategies

- **Uniswap**
    - **Overview**: Uniswap is one of the most popular decentralized exchanges (DEXs) that allows users to swap ERC-20 tokens. It uses an automated market maker (AMM) model where users provide liquidity to pools.
    - **Strategy**: Liquidity providers earn a portion of the trading fees generated by the pool. To maximize returns, investors can provide liquidity to pairs with high trading volumes and low volatility.
    - **Risks**: Exposure to impermanent loss and smart contract vulnerabilities.

- **Aave**
  - **Overview**: Aave is a decentralized lending platform where users can lend and borrow various cryptocurrencies. Lenders provide liquidity to pools and earn interest.
  - **Strategy**: By supplying stablecoins or other cryptocurrencies to Aave, users can earn interest paid by borrowers. Additionally, participating in Aave's liquidity mining programs can yield additional AAVE tokens.
  - **Risks**: Potential smart contract vulnerabilities and liquidity risks during high demand periods.
- **Compound**
  - **Overview**: Compound is another leading DeFi lending platform that allows users to supply and borrow assets. Suppliers earn interest on their deposits.
  - **Strategy**: Investors can supply assets like stablecoins to earn interest, and participate in liquidity mining to earn COMP tokens as additional rewards.
  - **Risks**: Similar to Aave, smart contract risks and potential liquidity issues during volatile market conditions.
- **SushiSwap**
  - **Overview**: SushiSwap is a decentralized exchange that operates similarly to Uniswap but offers additional features, including yield farming opportunities.
  - **Strategy**: Liquidity providers can earn trading fees and participate in yield farming by staking their LP tokens to earn SUSHI tokens. Combining LP

- - rewards and SUSHI farming can enhance returns.
  - **Risks**: Exposure to impermanent loss, smart contract vulnerabilities, and market volatility.
- **Balancer**
  - **Overview**: Balancer is a flexible AMM that allows users to create and manage liquidity pools with multiple tokens and varying weights.
  - **Strategy**: Liquidity providers can create customized pools to optimize returns and reduce impermanent loss. Balancer also offers BAL tokens as liquidity mining rewards.
  - **Risks**: Smart contract risks and the complexity of managing multi-asset pools.
- **Yearn.Finance**
  - **Overview**: Yearn.Finance is a yield aggregator that optimizes yield farming strategies across various DeFi protocols.
  - **Strategy**: Users can deposit their assets into Yearn vaults, which automatically move funds between different protocols to maximize yields. This simplifies the process for investors looking for high returns.
  - **Risks**: Reliance on multiple smart contracts, each with its own vulnerabilities, and the potential for complex strategies to fail.

Yield farming and liquidity mining have emerged as powerful strategies within the decentralized finance (DeFi) ecosystem, offering substantial rewards for those willing to navigate their complexities. By providing liquidity to DeFi protocols, investors can earn significant returns through transaction fees, interest, and token rewards. Platforms like

Uniswap, Aave, Compound, SushiSwap, Balancer, and Yearn.Finance present diverse opportunities to engage in these activities, each with unique mechanisms and benefits.

However, the allure of high returns comes with considerable risks. Smart contract vulnerabilities can lead to significant losses, as can impermanent loss, where the value of staked assets changes unfavourably. Additionally, regulatory uncertainties and market volatility add layers of risk that must be carefully managed.

To succeed in yield farming and liquidity mining, thorough research and a strategic approach are crucial. Investors should diversify their holdings, use well-audited platforms, and continuously monitor market conditions. By balancing the pursuit of high yields with prudent risk management, participants can effectively leverage the potential of DeFi to enhance their cryptocurrency portfolios.

In summary, yield farming and liquidity mining offer innovative ways to generate passive income and support the growth of decentralized finance. While they present opportunities for high rewards, they also require a deep understanding of the associated risks and a disciplined investment strategy. By staying informed and cautious, investors can navigate this dynamic landscape and achieve their financial goals.

Chapter 6: Mining

Basics of Cryptocurrency Mining

Cryptocurrency mining is the process by which new digital coins are created and transactions are verified and added to a blockchain. It is a crucial aspect of Proof of Work (PoW) cryptocurrencies like Bitcoin. Mining involves solving complex mathematical problems using computational power, a process known as hashing. Miners compete to solve these problems, and the first to do so gets to add a new block to the blockchain and is rewarded with newly created coins, along with transaction fees from the transactions included in the block. This process ensures the security and integrity of the blockchain, preventing double-spending and other fraudulent activities. Over time, as more coins are mined, the difficulty of these mathematical problems increases, requiring more advanced and powerful hardware to solve them.

Advantages

Earning New Coins

The primary advantage of cryptocurrency mining is the ability to earn new coins as a reward for validating transactions and securing the network. These mining rewards can be substantial, especially for early adopters or those mining highly valued cryptocurrencies. As the value of mined coins increases, the profitability of mining can also increase, making it a potentially lucrative activity. Additionally, miners receive transaction fees from the transactions they validate, providing another source of income.

Mining can also contribute to the decentralisation and security of a cryptocurrency network. By participating in the mining process, miners help distribute the network's processing power, making it more resistant to attacks and centralisation. This contribution is crucial for maintaining the integrity and resilience of the blockchain.

Mining provides a tangible way to support the underlying technology of cryptocurrencies. By validating transactions and adding them to the blockchain, miners ensure that the network remains secure and reliable. This not only protects the value of the cryptocurrency but also fosters trust and adoption by users and investors.

Risks

High Initial Investment and Ongoing Costs

Despite its potential rewards, cryptocurrency mining comes with significant risks, primarily related to the high initial investment and ongoing operational costs. Setting up a mining operation requires purchasing specialized hardware known as ASICs (Application-Specific Integrated Circuits) for Bitcoin or GPUs (Graphics Processing Units) for other cryptocurrencies. These devices can be expensive, with costs running into thousands of pounds.

In addition to the initial hardware costs, mining involves substantial ongoing expenses, particularly for electricity and cooling. Mining rigs consume a considerable amount of power, and the associated electricity costs can significantly impact profitability. Effective cooling solutions are also necessary to prevent overheating, which can damage hardware and reduce its lifespan.

Market volatility poses another risk. The profitability of mining is closely tied to the value of the mined cryptocurrency. If the market price of the coin falls, the rewards might not cover the operational costs, leading to financial losses. Moreover, mining difficulty—the complexity of the mathematical problems miners must solve—tends to increase over time as more miners join the network. This increase can reduce the number of coins mined, impacting overall profitability.

Regulatory risks also exist. Governments worldwide are still determining how to regulate cryptocurrencies and mining activities. Changes in regulation can affect the legality and financial viability of mining operations.

Mining hardware can become obsolete quickly. As technology advances, older mining equipment may no longer be efficient enough to compete with newer models. This obsolescence can force miners to continually invest in new hardware to maintain profitability, adding to the overall costs.

Environmental concerns are also a risk factor. The high energy consumption associated with mining has attracted scrutiny and criticism, particularly in regions where electricity is generated from non-renewable sources. This can lead to potential regulatory actions or increased electricity costs, further impacting the profitability of mining operations.

Mining Equipment and Setup

Hardware and Software Recommendations

Setting up a successful mining operation requires careful selection of hardware and software to maximize efficiency and profitability.

Hardware

- **ASICs (Application-Specific Integrated Circuits):** For Bitcoin and other PoW cryptocurrencies that require high computational power, ASIC miners are the preferred choice. They are optimized for specific algorithms, offering superior performance and energy efficiency compared to general-purpose hardware. Popular ASIC models include the Bitmain Antminer S19 Pro and the MicroBT WhatsMiner M30S. These machines are designed specifically for mining and can perform the required calculations much faster and more efficiently than other types of hardware.

- **GPUs (Graphics Processing Units)**: For mining cryptocurrencies like Ethereum, which are resistant to ASIC mining, GPUs are commonly used. High-performance GPUs such as the NVIDIA GeForce RTX 3080 and AMD Radeon RX 6800 XT are popular choices. GPUs are versatile and can be used to mine various altcoins, making them a flexible option. They are particularly useful for mining coins that use memory-intensive algorithms, which are less efficient on ASIC hardware.

- **CPUs (Central Processing Units)**: Although less efficient than ASICs and GPUs, CPUs can still be used for mining certain cryptocurrencies, particularly in the early stages of a coin's development. However, they are generally not recommended for serious mining operations due to their lower performance. CPUs are mainly used for mining new or niche cryptocurrencies where the competition is lower, and specialized hardware is not yet available.

- **Cooling Solutions**: Proper cooling is essential to maintain the performance and longevity of mining hardware. Air conditioning units, high-speed fans, and custom cooling systems can help manage the heat generated by mining rigs. Some advanced setups use liquid cooling systems to maintain optimal temperatures, which can enhance the efficiency and lifespan of the mining equipment.

- **Power Supply Units (PSUs)**: Reliable and efficient power supplies are crucial for mining operations. High-wattage

PSUs from reputable manufacturers ensure stable power delivery to your mining rigs. Overloading or using low-quality PSUs can lead to hardware failure or reduced efficiency.

Software

- **Mining Software**: The choice of mining software depends on the cryptocurrency being mined and the hardware used. Popular mining software includes CGMiner, BFGMiner, and EasyMiner for ASICs, and Ethminer, Claymore, and PhoenixMiner for GPUs. These programs connect miners to the blockchain network and manage the mining process, allowing users to monitor performance, temperatures, and profitability.

- **Mining Pools**: Joining a mining pool can increase the chances of earning rewards by combining the computational power of multiple miners. Popular mining pools include Slush Pool, F2Pool, and AntPool for Bitcoin, and Ethermine and SparkPool for Ethereum. Pools distribute rewards proportionally based on the contributed hash power, providing more consistent returns than solo mining. Participating in a pool reduces the variance of mining rewards, making income more predictable.

- **Wallets**: A secure cryptocurrency wallet is necessary to store mined coins. Hardware wallets like Ledger Nano S, Ledger Nano X, and Trezor offer high security. Software wallets like Exodus and Trust Wallet are also widely used. It is essential to choose a wallet that supports the cryptocurrency you are mining and provides robust security features to protect your assets.

- **Monitoring Software**: To optimize mining operations, monitoring software like Minerstat or Awesome Miner can be used. These tools provide real-time data on mining performance, temperature, power consumption, and profitability, allowing miners to make informed decisions and adjustments.

Setup

- **Electricity Supply**: Ensure a reliable and sufficient electricity supply to power the mining rigs. Consider the cost of electricity in your location, as it can significantly impact profitability. Some miners set up operations in regions with lower electricity costs to maximize returns.
- **Internet Connection**: A stable and fast internet connection is essential for efficient mining operations. Downtime or slow connections can reduce mining efficiency and profitability. A wired connection is preferable to minimize latency and ensure consistent data transmission.
- **Location**: Choose a suitable location with adequate ventilation and cooling to prevent overheating. Noise levels from cooling systems and mining rigs should also be considered. Industrial spaces, basements, or dedicated mining facilities are often used to accommodate the equipment and manage noise and heat.
- **Security**: Implement physical and cybersecurity measures to protect mining equipment and digital assets. This includes securing the location with locks and surveillance, using firewalls, and keeping software up to date. Regular backups of wallet data and using multi-factor authentication can further enhance security.
- **Environmental Considerations**: Address environmental concerns by exploring renewable energy options or implementing energy-efficient practices. Some miners use solar or wind power to reduce their carbon footprint and

lower electricity costs.

In conclusion, cryptocurrency mining is a complex but potentially rewarding activity that involves significant investment and operational considerations. By understanding the basics, advantages, risks, and best practices for equipment and setup, aspiring miners can make informed decisions and optimize their chances for success in the dynamic world of cryptocurrency mining. Proper planning, risk management, and continuous adaptation to technological advancements are key to maintaining profitability and contributing to the security and decentralization of blockchain networks.

Chapter 7: Participating in Initial Coin Offerings (ICOs) and Token Sales

What are ICOs and Token Sales?

Initial Coin Offerings (ICOs) and token sales are fundraising mechanisms used by blockchain-based projects to raise capital. These methods have become popular ways for startups to bypass traditional venture capital funding and connect directly with potential users and investors. In an ICO, a new cryptocurrency project sells a portion of its native tokens to early investors in exchange for established cryptocurrencies like Bitcoin or Ethereum, or sometimes fiat currency. Token sales can take various forms, including public sales, private sales, and presales, each with specific conditions and price points. The primary goal is to secure funding for project development, marketing, and operational expenses.

ICOs gained prominence with the success of Ethereum's ICO in 2014, which raised $18 million over 42 days. Since then, countless projects have used this model to launch their tokens and build their ecosystems. Tokens sold during an ICO can represent various forms of value or utility within the project's ecosystem, such as access to a platform, voting rights, or potential future returns. These tokens are typically created on a blockchain platform like Ethereum, using standards such as ERC-20 for fungible tokens or ERC-721 for non-fungible tokens (NFTs).

Advantages

Early Investment Opportunities

Participating in ICOs and token sales offers several advantages, particularly the opportunity to invest early in promising projects. Early investors can purchase tokens at a lower price before they are listed on public exchanges. If the project succeeds, the value of these tokens can increase significantly, leading to substantial returns on investment. This early entry can be particularly lucrative in a rapidly evolving market, where successful projects can achieve exponential growth.

For instance, early participants in Ethereum's ICO have seen their investments grow manifold as Ethereum became a cornerstone of the blockchain ecosystem. Similar success stories include projects like Binance Coin (BNB) and Chainlink (LINK), which have provided early investors with substantial returns.

Another advantage is the ability to diversify an investment portfolio. ICOs and token sales provide access to a wide range of projects across various sectors, from finance and gaming to healthcare and supply chain management. This diversification can mitigate risks and increase the potential for high returns.

Investors also have the opportunity to support innovative and disruptive technologies. By participating in ICOs and token sales, investors can contribute to the development of projects that have the potential to transform industries and create new value propositions. This involvement can be both financially rewarding and personally satisfying, as investors become part of a growing and dynamic ecosystem.

Additionally, ICOs often offer bonus tokens or discounts to early investors, providing further incentives to participate early. These bonuses can significantly enhance the overall return on investment if the project succeeds.

Risks

Scams and Regulatory Issues

Despite the potential rewards, participating in ICOs and token sales comes with significant risks. One of the primary risks is the prevalence of scams and fraudulent projects. The relatively unregulated nature of the ICO space has made it a target for unscrupulous actors looking to exploit investors. Scams can take various forms, from outright fraud where project founders disappear with the funds to more subtle deceptions involving unrealistic promises and misleading information.

The infamous case of BitConnect, which was exposed as a Ponzi scheme, serves as a stark reminder of the risks involved. Investors lost billions when the platform collapsed, highlighting the importance of thorough due diligence.

Regulatory issues also pose a substantial risk. Governments and regulatory bodies worldwide are still determining how to regulate ICOs and token sales. Regulatory changes can impact the legality and financial viability of these projects. For instance, a project that complies with regulations in one jurisdiction might face legal challenges in another, potentially affecting the project's ability to operate and deliver on its promises.

In 2017, the U.S. Securities and Exchange Commission (SEC) declared that many ICOs were actually offering securities and thus subject to federal securities laws. This led to increased scrutiny and several enforcement actions against non-compliant ICOs.

Market volatility is another risk factor. The value of tokens acquired during an ICO or token sale can fluctuate dramatically once they are listed on public exchanges. Market conditions, investor sentiment, and the project's performance can all influence token prices, leading to potential losses. For example, during the crypto market downturn of

2018, many ICO tokens lost significant value, leaving investors with substantial losses.

How to Evaluate ICOs

Key Factors and Red Flags

Evaluating ICOs and token sales requires careful analysis to identify legitimate and promising projects while avoiding scams. Here are key factors to consider and red flags to watch out for:

1. Team and Advisors

- **Key Factors**: Research the project's team members and advisors. Look for individuals with relevant experience, a solid track record, and a positive reputation in the blockchain and cryptocurrency space. Transparent and accessible team information is a good sign. For example, a team that has successfully launched previous blockchain projects or has a background in technology and finance adds credibility.
- **Red Flags**: Anonymous team members, lack of relevant experience, or a history of involvement in failed or fraudulent projects should raise concerns. If the team members' credentials cannot be verified or if they have been linked to previous scams, it's best to stay away.

2. Whitepaper and Roadmap

- **Key Factors**: A comprehensive and well-written whitepaper should clearly outline the project's goals, technology, use cases, and tokenomics. A detailed roadmap with realistic milestones indicates a well-planned project. The whitepaper should provide technical details, problem-solving strategies, and a clear vision for the project's future.

- **Red Flags**: Vague, poorly written, or overly technical whitepapers can be a sign of a poorly thought-out project. Unrealistic or overly ambitious roadmaps are also a warning sign. If the whitepaper lacks clarity or avoids addressing critical issues, it might be an indication of a potential scam.

3. Technology and Use Case

- **Key Factors**: Assess the technology behind the project and its proposed use case. The project should solve a real problem or offer a unique value proposition. Look for working prototypes or beta versions that demonstrate the project's viability. The technology stack, including the blockchain platform, consensus mechanism, and any proprietary innovations, should be robust and well-documented.
- **Red Flags**: Projects with no clear use case, no working product, or those that seem to rely on buzzwords without substance should be approached with caution. Overpromising on technological capabilities without evidence is a major red flag.

4. Community and Partnerships

- **Key Factors**: A strong and active community can indicate genuine interest and support for the project. Partnerships with reputable companies and organizations add credibility. Active participation on social media, forums, and other platforms can provide insights into the project's engagement and transparency.
- **Red Flags**: Lack of community engagement, minimal social media presence, or partnerships with unknown or dubious entities are red flags. If the project's social media accounts

have low engagement or are filled with bots, it suggests a lack of genuine interest.

5. Tokenomics and Distribution

- **Key Factors**: Understand the tokenomics, including the total supply, distribution model, and use of funds. Tokens should have a clear utility within the project's ecosystem. A fair distribution model ensures that no single entity holds too much power or influence over the project.
- **Red Flags**: Unfair token distribution, where the majority of tokens are allocated to the team or advisors, or a lack of transparency in how funds will be used, can be problematic. Excessive token allocations to insiders can lead to market manipulation and rapid sell-offs.

6. Legal and Regulatory Compliance

- **Key Factors**: Ensure the project complies with relevant regulations in its jurisdiction. Look for legal opinions or audits that confirm compliance. Projects that proactively address regulatory issues and operate transparently are more likely to succeed.
- **Red Flags**: Projects that avoid discussing regulatory compliance or operate in jurisdictions with unclear or unfavourable regulations may pose significant risks. Non-compliance with local laws can result in legal actions and project shutdowns.

7. Security Measures

- **Key Factors**: Evaluate the security measures in place to protect investors' funds and data. Regular security audits and bug bounty programs are positive indicators. Projects should prioritize security in their development process and engage third-party security firms for assessments.

- **Red Flags**: Projects with a history of security breaches, no mention of security protocols, or those that do not prioritize security are risky investments. Lack of transparency about security practices can indicate potential vulnerabilities.

8. Transparency and Communication

- **Key Factors**: Transparent communication from the project team, including regular updates and open channels for investor inquiries, is crucial. Projects that maintain active communication with their community and provide regular progress reports are more likely to be trustworthy.
- **Red Flags**: Projects that are opaque about their progress, avoid questions, or provide inconsistent information should be approached with caution. Poor communication can signal underlying issues or a lack of commitment.

By considering these key factors and being vigilant for red flags, investors can make more informed decisions when participating in ICOs and token sales. Conducting thorough due diligence and seeking independent advice can further mitigate risks and increase the likelihood of investing in successful and legitimate projects.

Conclusion

Participating in Initial Coin Offerings (ICOs) and token sales offers investors the chance to get in early on innovative blockchain projects with the potential for high returns. Success stories like Ethereum's ICO illustrate how early investments can yield substantial gains as projects grow and thrive. This opportunity to buy tokens at a lower price before they hit public exchanges is a major draw for many investors.

However, these opportunities come with significant risks. The unregulated nature of the ICO space has led to numerous scams and fraudulent projects. High-profile cases like BitConnect have shown the dangers of investing in poorly vetted schemes, highlighting the importance of thorough due diligence. Investors must scrutinize project teams, whitepapers, roadmaps, technology, community engagement, partnerships, tokenomics, and regulatory compliance to identify legitimate and promising projects.

Regulatory issues add another layer of complexity. Governments are still developing frameworks for regulating ICOs, leading to legal uncertainties that can affect project viability. The U.S. Securities and Exchange Commission's classification of many ICOs as securities has resulted in increased scrutiny and enforcement actions, impacting investor returns.

Market volatility is another inherent risk. The value of ICO tokens can fluctuate dramatically once listed on public exchanges, influenced by market sentiment, broader cryptocurrency trends, and the specific project's performance. The 2018 crypto market downturn, where many ICO tokens lost significant value, underscores the need for effective risk management strategies.

To evaluate ICOs effectively, investors should consider factors such as the experience and credibility of the team, the clarity and feasibility of the whitepaper, the technology and use case, community engagement, partnerships, tokenomics, and security measures. Transparent communication and regular updates from the project team are also crucial for building trust and demonstrating commitment.

In summary, while ICOs and token sales present exciting investment opportunities, they also come with substantial risks. By conducting thorough due diligence, staying informed about regulatory developments, and critically evaluating projects, investors can navigate the ICO landscape more effectively. This diligent approach helps maximize potential returns while minimizing exposure to scams and regulatory pitfalls. Balancing caution with informed optimism allows investors to leverage the transformative potential of ICOs and token sales, contributing to the growth of groundbreaking technologies and potentially achieving significant financial gains.

Chapter 8: Arbitrage

Exploiting Price Differences Across Exchanges

Arbitrage in the context of cryptocurrency trading involves exploiting the price differences of a specific cryptocurrency across different exchanges. Since cryptocurrency markets are decentralized and operate independently, the price of a given digital asset can vary from one exchange to another. Arbitrage traders capitalize on these discrepancies by buying the asset at a lower price on one exchange and simultaneously selling it at a higher price on another, thus making a profit from the price differential. This strategy relies on the ability to execute trades quickly and efficiently, ensuring that the price difference covers transaction costs and provides a net profit.

Arbitrage can take several forms, including spatial arbitrage, where the trader moves funds between different exchanges, and triangular arbitrage, which involves exploiting price differences among three different trading pairs. Both methods require careful planning, swift execution, and effective management of trading accounts across multiple platforms.

Advantages

Low Risk if Executed Properly

One of the primary advantages of arbitrage trading is its relatively low risk, provided it is executed properly. Since arbitrage takes advantage of existing price discrepancies rather than relying on market trends or predictions, it can be less exposed to market volatility. The profit margins in arbitrage are typically small but consistent, making it a strategy focused on steady, incremental gains rather than high-risk, high-reward trading.

Arbitrage trading does not require long-term holding of assets, thereby reducing exposure to market downturns. By quickly moving assets in and out of exchanges, traders can mitigate the risks associated with price fluctuations over time. Additionally, arbitrage opportunities are often more predictable and quantifiable, making them an attractive option for traders looking for a systematic and reliable profit strategy.

Furthermore, arbitrage trading can be automated using trading bots and algorithms, which can identify and exploit price discrepancies much faster than a human trader. This automation can further reduce the risk by ensuring that trades are executed promptly and accurately, taking advantage of fleeting arbitrage opportunities.

Risks

Transfer Times and Fees

Despite its advantages, arbitrage trading is not without risks. One of the primary challenges is the transfer time between exchanges. Cryptocurrencies can take varying amounts of time to be transferred from one exchange to another, depending on network congestion and the specific blockchain's transaction speed. During this transfer time, the price difference may diminish or disappear, turning a potentially profitable trade into a loss.

Transaction fees are another significant factor that can impact the profitability of arbitrage trading. Each transaction, whether it's buying, selling, or transferring assets, incurs fees that can eat into the profit margins. It's crucial to account for these fees when calculating potential profits to ensure that the arbitrage opportunity is indeed worthwhile.

Market liquidity also poses a risk. If the trading volume on either exchange is low, executing large trades without significant price slippage can be challenging. Slippage occurs when the execution of a large order causes the asset's price to move unfavorably, reducing the expected profit.

Additionally, regulatory differences between exchanges located in different countries can introduce compliance risks. Traders must ensure that they adhere to the legal and regulatory requirements of each exchange to avoid potential legal issues.

Tools and Techniques

Platforms and Strategies for Effective Arbitrage

To effectively engage in arbitrage trading, traders need access to several tools and platforms that can streamline the process and increase the likelihood of success.

1. Arbitrage Bots and Software

- **HaasOnline**: This trading platform offers advanced arbitrage bots that can automate the detection and execution of arbitrage opportunities across multiple exchanges.
- **Gimmer**: A platform that provides customizable trading bots, including those designed for arbitrage, which can operate across different exchanges.
- **CryptoHopper**: This service offers a range of trading bots with arbitrage capabilities, allowing traders to automate their strategies and take advantage of price discrepancies efficiently.

2. Real-Time Data and Alerts

- **CoinMarketCap and CoinGecko**: These websites provide

real-time price data for various cryptocurrencies across multiple exchanges. Setting up alerts for specific price movements can help traders quickly identify arbitrage opportunities.

- **ArbiTool**: A specialized tool that monitors multiple exchanges for price differences and alerts traders to potential arbitrage opportunities.

3. Multi-Exchange Accounts

- Maintaining accounts on multiple cryptocurrency exchanges is essential for arbitrage trading. This setup allows traders to quickly execute trades without the delay of setting up new accounts or transferring funds between platforms.
- Popular exchanges for arbitrage include Binance, Kraken, Bitfinex, and Coinbase Pro, each offering a wide range of trading pairs and high liquidity.

4. Triangular Arbitrage

- This strategy involves exploiting price differences between three different trading pairs within a single exchange. For example, a trader might identify a discrepancy between BTC/USD, USD/ETH, and ETH/BTC pairs. By cycling through these trades, the trader can lock in profits without moving funds between exchanges.
- Automated bots can be particularly effective for triangular arbitrage, as they can quickly calculate and execute the necessary trades to capture the price differences.

5. Spatial Arbitrage

- Spatial arbitrage requires moving funds between different

exchanges to exploit price differences. This method involves a thorough understanding of transfer times and fees associated with moving assets between platforms.

- Ensuring sufficient balance on each exchange to cover potential arbitrage trades can reduce the need for constant fund transfers, thereby minimizing transfer times and associated risks.

6. Risk Management

- Effective risk management strategies are crucial for successful arbitrage trading. This includes setting clear profit targets, using stop-loss orders to limit potential losses, and continuously monitoring the market for changes that might impact arbitrage opportunities.
- Diversifying arbitrage strategies across different cryptocurrencies and exchanges can also help mitigate risks and ensure more consistent returns.

Conclusion

Arbitrage trading stands out as a sophisticated and potentially profitable strategy within the cryptocurrency market, offering traders a way to capitalize on price discrepancies across various exchanges. This method leverages the inherent inefficiencies in a decentralized and fragmented market, turning these gaps into opportunities for consistent returns. However, like any trading strategy, arbitrage requires a deep understanding of market mechanics, meticulous planning, and effective execution to maximize its benefits and minimize associated risks.

The primary allure of arbitrage trading lies in its relatively low-risk profile. Unlike speculative trading strategies that depend on market trends and future price movements, arbitrage is based on existing price differentials. This reduces the exposure to market volatility and allows traders to generate steady, incremental profits. The ability to automate arbitrage processes through advanced trading bots further enhances this strategy's attractiveness, enabling traders to quickly and efficiently exploit fleeting price discrepancies without the need for constant manual intervention.

Despite its advantages, arbitrage is not without challenges. One of the most significant hurdles is the time required to transfer assets between exchanges. Cryptocurrency transactions can vary in speed depending on network congestion and the blockchain protocol used. Delays in transfers can erode potential profits as price differences narrow, turning a seemingly profitable trade into a loss. Therefore, it is crucial for traders to consider transfer times and opt for cryptocurrencies and exchanges that offer faster transaction processing.

Transaction fees also play a critical role in determining the profitability of arbitrage trades. Each trade incurs costs, including trading fees on both exchanges and transfer fees for moving assets. High fees can quickly diminish the margins of arbitrage opportunities. As such, traders must carefully calculate all associated costs to ensure that the net profit remains favourable. Choosing exchanges with competitive fee structures and leveraging any available discounts or rebates can help mitigate these costs.

Market liquidity is another essential factor in successful arbitrage trading. High liquidity ensures that traders can execute large trades without significantly impacting the asset's price. Low liquidity, on the other hand, can lead to price slippage, where the execution price differs from the expected price, reducing potential profits. Selecting exchanges known for high trading volumes and liquidity can help minimize this risk and ensure smoother execution of arbitrage trades.

Regulatory considerations also cannot be overlooked. Cryptocurrency regulations vary widely across different jurisdictions, and compliance with these regulations is paramount to avoid legal complications. Traders must stay informed about the regulatory environment of the exchanges they use and ensure that their trading activities comply with local laws. This includes understanding any tax implications and reporting requirements associated with arbitrage trading.

To effectively engage in arbitrage, traders need a robust set of tools and platforms. Automated trading bots such as HaasOnline, Gimmer, and CryptoHopper can rapidly identify and act on arbitrage opportunities, significantly enhancing efficiency. Real-time data and alert systems from platforms like CoinMarketCap, CoinGecko, and ArbiTool provide the necessary information to spot price discrepancies quickly. Maintaining accounts on multiple exchanges, such as Binance, Kraken, Bitfinex, and Coinbase Pro, ensures readiness to execute trades swiftly and capitalize on arbitrage opportunities as they arise.

Arbitrage strategies can be further refined through techniques like triangular arbitrage, which involves exploiting price differences between three different trading pairs within a single exchange. This method circumvents the need for cross-exchange transfers, thereby reducing transfer times and fees. Spatial arbitrage, which requires moving funds between different exchanges, demands a thorough understanding of the associated logistics and costs but can be highly profitable when executed correctly.

Effective risk management is vital for sustained success in arbitrage trading. This includes setting clear profit targets, using stop-loss orders to limit potential losses, and continuously monitoring market conditions. Diversifying arbitrage activities across various cryptocurrencies and exchanges can also help spread risk and ensure more consistent returns.

In summary, arbitrage trading offers a compelling avenue for profiting from the inefficiencies of the cryptocurrency market. While it presents challenges such as transfer times, transaction fees, liquidity issues, and regulatory considerations, these can be managed with careful planning, the right tools, and effective risk management strategies. By leveraging automation, real-time data, and maintaining readiness across multiple platforms, traders can capitalize on price discrepancies to achieve steady, incremental gains. As the cryptocurrency market continues to evolve, those who master the art of arbitrage trading will be well-positioned to reap its rewards, turning market inefficiencies into opportunities for profit.

Chapter 9: Airdrops and Forks

Receiving Free Tokens

Airdrops and forks are two mechanisms by which cryptocurrency users can receive free tokens. An airdrop involves distributing free tokens to holders of a particular cryptocurrency, often as part of a marketing strategy to increase awareness and adoption of a new token. This distribution can be based on various criteria, such as holding a specific amount of a given cryptocurrency at a particular snapshot in time or participating in a project's community activities. Airdrops can also reward users for supporting or promoting the project on social media platforms or engaging in specific activities such as signing up for newsletters.

Forks, on the other hand, occur when a blockchain splits into two separate chains. This split can result from disagreements within the community regarding the blockchain's development direction or to implement new features or updates. When a fork happens, holders of the original cryptocurrency typically receive an equivalent amount of the new cryptocurrency on the forked chain. There are two main types of forks: hard forks and soft forks. Hard forks create a completely new blockchain and cryptocurrency, while soft forks are backward-compatible updates to the existing blockchain.

Advantages

Free Assets

One of the primary advantages of airdrops and forks is that they provide users with free assets. This can be an excellent way for cryptocurrency holders to increase their portfolios without additional investment. For instance, when Bitcoin Cash (BCH) forked from Bitcoin (BTC) in 2017, Bitcoin holders received an equal amount of Bitcoin Cash, effectively doubling the number of tokens they held without spending any additional money.

Airdrops can also serve as an introduction to new projects and tokens. By distributing free tokens, projects can quickly build a user base and encourage engagement within their communities. For recipients, airdrops provide an opportunity to explore new projects and potentially profit from the tokens if they appreciate in value.

Moreover, airdrops and forks can serve as a reward for loyal community members and early adopters. They can incentivize users to hold onto their cryptocurrencies and participate more actively in the community. This can foster a sense of loyalty and support for the project, helping it grow and succeed.

Risks

Low or Volatile Value

While airdrops and forks offer free tokens, these tokens often come with risks, primarily related to their value. Many airdropped tokens may have little to no value initially and can be highly volatile. The value of these tokens can fluctuate significantly, sometimes dropping sharply after the initial distribution. In some cases, tokens received from airdrops may never gain substantial value, resulting in negligible financial benefits for the holders.

Another risk is the potential for scams and fraudulent airdrops. Scammers may use the promise of free tokens to trick users into providing private information or transferring funds. It is crucial to exercise caution and conduct thorough research before participating in any airdrop.

Additionally, forks can create confusion and uncertainty within the cryptocurrency community. The creation of a new cryptocurrency can lead to disagreements and conflicts, affecting the value and stability of the original cryptocurrency. Users must stay informed about the developments and implications of forks to make informed decisions about their holdings.

Tax implications are another consideration. In many jurisdictions, receiving free tokens through airdrops or forks may be considered taxable income. This means that recipients might need to report the value of the received tokens and pay taxes on them, even if they do not sell the tokens immediately. It is important to understand the tax regulations in your area and comply with any reporting requirements.

How to Find Airdrops

Platforms and Methods to Participate

Finding and participating in airdrops can be a rewarding experience if done correctly. Several platforms and methods can help users identify legitimate airdrops and take part in them.

1. Airdrop Aggregator Websites

- **Airdrop Alert**: A popular platform that lists upcoming and ongoing airdrops. It provides detailed information about each airdrop, including participation requirements and steps to claim the tokens.
- **Airdrops.io**: Another well-known aggregator that offers a comprehensive list of airdrops. The platform categorizes airdrops based on various criteria, making it easy for users to find suitable opportunities.
- **CoinMarketCap Airdrops**: CoinMarketCap, a leading cryptocurrency data provider, also features a section

dedicated to airdrops. Users can find airdrop campaigns from various projects and participate directly through the platform.

2. Social Media and Forums

- **Twitter**: Many cryptocurrency projects announce airdrops on their official Twitter accounts. Following these accounts and keeping an eye on relevant hashtags (#airdrop, #cryptoairdrop) can help users stay updated.
- **Reddit**: Subreddits like r/cryptocurrency and r/airdropalert often feature posts about upcoming airdrops. Engaging with these communities can provide valuable insights and alerts.

3. Project Websites and Newsletters

- Many blockchain projects announce airdrops on their official websites and through newsletters. Subscribing to newsletters from projects you are interested in can ensure you receive timely information about airdrops.

4. Cryptocurrency Wallets

- Some cryptocurrency wallets, like Trust Wallet and Atomic Wallet, feature integrated airdrop sections where users can find and participate in airdrops directly from their wallets. This integration simplifies the process and adds a layer of security.

5. Telegram Groups and Channels

- Telegram is a popular platform for cryptocurrency communities. Many projects have official Telegram groups or channels where they announce airdrops. Joining these groups can provide direct access to airdrop information and community discussions.

6. Airdrop Bounty Programs

- Some projects offer bounty programs where users can earn additional tokens by completing specific tasks, such as promoting the project on social media, writing articles, or translating content. Participating in these programs can provide more substantial rewards than standard airdrops.

How to Participate in Airdrops

- **Wallet Address**: Ensure you have a compatible cryptocurrency wallet to receive the airdropped tokens. Most airdrops require an Ethereum wallet address, as many tokens are ERC-20 based.
- **Social Media Engagement**: Follow the project's social media accounts, join their communities, and engage as required. Tasks may include retweeting, sharing posts, or tagging friends.
- **Sign-Up and Verification**: Some airdrops require users to sign up on the project's website and complete a verification process, which may include KYC (Know Your Customer) checks.
- **Referral Programs**: Many airdrops offer additional tokens for referring friends. Share your referral link to increase your airdrop rewards.

Conclusion

Airdrops and forks represent intriguing aspects of the cryptocurrency world, providing users with opportunities to receive free tokens and expand their investment portfolios without any additional financial outlay. These mechanisms not only help in broadening the adoption of new cryptocurrencies but also offer tangible benefits to the recipients, fostering a more engaged and supportive community around the projects.

The primary allure of airdrops and forks lies in the ability to obtain free assets. For many cryptocurrency enthusiasts, the chance to receive new tokens simply by holding an existing cryptocurrency or by participating in a project's community is a significant incentive. This has proven effective for many projects, helping them to quickly build a user base and gain traction in a competitive market. For recipients, these tokens can provide an introduction to new projects and potentially substantial profits if the tokens appreciate in value.

However, the excitement surrounding airdrops and forks must be tempered with an understanding of the associated risks. One of the main challenges is the often volatile nature of the value of the received tokens. While some tokens may experience significant appreciation, others may quickly lose value or never achieve substantial market presence. This volatility can affect the perceived benefits of the tokens and influence the decision of whether to hold or sell them.

Scams and fraudulent airdrops present another significant risk. The promise of free tokens can be exploited by malicious actors to trick users into providing private information or transferring funds. It is crucial to exercise caution and conduct thorough research before participating in any airdrop or fork. Only engage with reputable projects and platforms to minimize the risk of falling victim to scams.

Regulatory considerations also play a vital role in the realm of airdrops and forks. In many jurisdictions, receiving free tokens through these mechanisms can be considered taxable events, with recipients required to report the value of the tokens and potentially pay taxes on them. Understanding and complying with local tax regulations is essential to avoid legal issues and ensure that any financial benefits from airdrops and forks are not offset by unexpected tax liabilities.

Despite these risks, there are effective strategies and tools available to help users find and participate in legitimate airdrops. Airdrop aggregator websites, such as Airdrop Alert, Airdrops.io, and CoinMarketCap Airdrops, provide comprehensive listings of upcoming and ongoing airdrops, along with detailed information on participation requirements. Social media platforms, especially Twitter and Reddit, are valuable resources for staying updated on new airdrop announcements and community discussions. Additionally, subscribing to project newsletters, joining official Telegram groups, and using cryptocurrency wallets with integrated airdrop features can enhance the ability to participate in these opportunities.

Participating in forks can also be rewarding but requires a clear understanding of the technical and community implications. Hard forks, which create entirely new blockchains and cryptocurrencies, often lead to debates and conflicts within the original community. Staying informed about the developments leading to a fork and understanding the positions of key stakeholders can help users make informed decisions about their holdings.

In summary, airdrops and forks offer unique and potentially lucrative opportunities for cryptocurrency users to receive free tokens and engage with new projects. While the potential for free assets is appealing, it is essential to be aware of the associated risks, including low or volatile token values, scams, and regulatory issues. By utilizing reliable platforms and methods to find and participate in airdrops, and by staying informed about forks, users can maximize their chances of benefiting from these opportunities. Careful research, cautious participation, and compliance with regulatory requirements will help users navigate the dynamic landscape of airdrops and forks effectively, making the most of the free assets they receive and contributing to the growth and success of the cryptocurrency ecosystem.

Chapter 10: Building and Investing in Crypto Startups

———

Developing or Investing in Blockchain Technologies

Building and investing in crypto startups involves engaging with innovative blockchain technologies and their applications. These startups focus on developing new cryptocurrencies, decentralized applications (dApps), smart contract platforms, and other blockchain-based solutions that aim to revolutionize various industries, from finance and supply chain management to healthcare and gaming. Entrepreneurs create these startups by leveraging blockchain's decentralized, transparent, and secure nature to address specific problems or improve existing processes. Investors, on the other hand, provide the necessary capital to support the development and growth of these startups in exchange for equity or tokens that can appreciate in value as the startup succeeds.

Developing a crypto startup typically involves a combination of technical expertise, strategic planning, and business acumen. Founders need to identify a compelling use case for blockchain technology, build a team of skilled professionals, and create a viable product or service. They must also navigate the regulatory landscape, secure funding, and market their project effectively to attract users and investors.

Investing in crypto startups offers an alternative approach to participating in the blockchain revolution. Investors can support promising projects at an early stage, often through venture capital, Initial Coin Offerings (ICOs), Security Token Offerings (STOs), or private sales. Successful investments can yield significant returns, but they also come with considerable risks.

Advantages

High Potential Returns, Diversification

One of the most significant advantages of building or investing in crypto startups is the potential for high returns. The blockchain industry is still in its early stages, and many successful projects have seen exponential growth in a relatively short period. Early investors in projects like Bitcoin, Ethereum, and Binance have reaped substantial profits as these startups evolved into major players in the crypto space. The high potential returns make crypto startups an attractive option for entrepreneurs and investors looking to capitalize on the burgeoning blockchain industry.

Diversification is another key advantage. Investing in a range of crypto startups allows investors to spread their risk across multiple projects and sectors. This diversified approach can mitigate the impact of any single project's failure on the overall investment portfolio. By backing various startups, investors can gain exposure to different blockchain applications and technologies, increasing the likelihood of benefiting from the industry's overall growth.

For entrepreneurs, building a crypto startup offers the opportunity to innovate and create solutions that can disrupt traditional industries. The decentralized nature of blockchain technology allows startups to operate with fewer intermediaries, reducing costs and increasing efficiency. This innovation can lead to the development of new business models and revenue streams, providing a competitive edge in the market.

Risks

High Failure Rate, Substantial Investment

Despite the potential rewards, building and investing in crypto startups come with significant risks. One of the primary challenges is the high failure rate of startups in general, which is also true for crypto startups. Many projects fail to gain traction due to various factors such as inadequate market demand, regulatory hurdles, technical issues, or poor management. The nascent nature of the blockchain industry means that it is highly competitive and rapidly evolving, making it difficult for startups to sustain long-term success.

Substantial investment is often required to build or support a crypto startup. Developing a blockchain project involves significant costs, including hiring skilled developers, conducting security audits, marketing, and legal compliance. These expenses can add up quickly, and there is no guarantee that the startup will generate sufficient revenue to cover them. For investors, this means that substantial capital is at risk, and they may need to provide additional funding to support the startup through its development stages.

Regulatory uncertainty is another critical risk. The regulatory environment for cryptocurrencies and blockchain technologies varies widely across jurisdictions and is continually evolving. Startups must navigate complex and often ambiguous regulations, which can impact their operations and potential for growth. Compliance with these regulations can be costly and time-consuming, and failure to comply can result in legal penalties or shutdowns.

Market volatility also poses a risk to crypto startups and their investors. The value of cryptocurrencies and blockchain assets can fluctuate dramatically, influenced by factors such as market sentiment, technological developments, and regulatory news. This volatility can affect the startup's funding, operational costs, and overall stability.

Success Stories

Examples of Successful Crypto Startups

Despite the risks, there are several notable success stories in the crypto startup space that highlight the potential for substantial rewards. These examples demonstrate how innovative blockchain projects can achieve significant growth and impact various industries.

1. **Bitcoin (BTC)**
   - **Overview**: Launched in 2009 by an anonymous person or group known as Satoshi Nakamoto, Bitcoin is the first and most well-known cryptocurrency. It introduced the concept of a decentralized digital currency, secured by a blockchain.
   - **Success**: Bitcoin's value has grown exponentially since its inception, reaching all-time highs above $60,000 per BTC. It has achieved widespread adoption as a store of value and medium of exchange, inspiring the creation of thousands of other cryptocurrencies.
2. **Ethereum (ETH)**
   - **Overview**: Launched in 2015 by Vitalik Buterin and a team of co-founders, Ethereum is a decentralized platform that enables the creation of smart contracts and decentralized applications (dApps). Its native cryptocurrency, Ether, is used to power transactions and computations on the network.
   - **Success**: Ethereum has become the leading platform for blockchain innovation, hosting thousands of dApps and DeFi projects. Its market capitalization has grown significantly, making it the second-largest

cryptocurrency after Bitcoin.

3. **Binance (BNB)**

    - **Overview**: Founded in 2017 by Changpeng Zhao (CZ), Binance is one of the world's largest cryptocurrency exchanges. Binance Coin (BNB) is its native token, used to pay for transaction fees and participate in various activities on the platform.

    - **Success**: Binance quickly rose to prominence due to its wide range of supported cryptocurrencies, low fees, and user-friendly interface. BNB has appreciated substantially in value, and Binance has expanded its services to include DeFi, staking, and a smart contract platform, Binance Smart Chain.

4. **Chainlink (LINK)**

    - **Overview**: Chainlink, launched in 2017, is a decentralized oracle network that enables smart contracts to securely interact with real-world data. It was founded by Sergey Nazarov and Steve Ellis.

    - **Success**: Chainlink has become a crucial component of the blockchain ecosystem, providing reliable data feeds to various DeFi projects and smart contracts. LINK, its native token, has seen significant price appreciation, reflecting its growing utility and adoption.

5. **Uniswap (UNI)**

    - **Overview**: Uniswap, launched in 2018 by Hayden Adams, is a decentralized exchange (DEX) that uses an automated market maker (AMM) model to facilitate trading of ERC-20 tokens. Its native token, UNI, is used for governance and staking.

    - **Success**: Uniswap revolutionized the DEX

landscape by providing a seamless and decentralized trading experience. It has become one of the most popular DEXs, with substantial trading volumes and liquidity. UNI has appreciated in value as Uniswap's adoption has grown.

Conclusion

Building and investing in crypto startups represents a high-stakes, high-reward venture within the burgeoning blockchain and cryptocurrency ecosystem. The appeal of substantial returns and the potential to be part of revolutionary technological advancements drive both entrepreneurs and investors towards this dynamic field. However, success in this arena requires a deep understanding of the unique challenges and risks associated with blockchain technology and the volatile cryptocurrency market.

One of the most compelling advantages of engaging with crypto startups is the opportunity for high potential returns. The rapid growth of successful projects like Bitcoin, Ethereum, Binance, Chainlink, and Uniswap demonstrates the financial rewards that can be achieved. Early investors in these projects have seen exponential gains, reflecting the immense value that innovative blockchain solutions can bring to various sectors. For entrepreneurs, creating a successful crypto startup offers the chance to disrupt traditional industries, introduce new business models, and establish a lasting impact on the global economy.

Diversification is another significant benefit. By investing in a range of crypto startups, investors can spread their risk across multiple projects and sectors, enhancing the potential for consistent returns. This diversified approach can mitigate the impact of any single project's failure and increase exposure to the broader growth of the blockchain industry. For startups, leveraging diverse applications of blockchain technology can attract a wider audience and create multiple revenue streams, contributing to long-term sustainability.

Despite these promising advantages, the risks associated with building and investing in crypto startups are substantial. The high failure rate of startups, compounded by the competitive and rapidly evolving nature of the blockchain industry, means that many projects struggle to achieve lasting success. Entrepreneurs must navigate technical challenges, secure adequate funding, and manage regulatory compliance while building a viable product. Investors face the risk of substantial financial loss if a startup fails to deliver on its promises or if market conditions deteriorate.

Regulatory uncertainty further complicates the landscape. Different jurisdictions have varying approaches to regulating cryptocurrencies and blockchain technologies, and these regulations are continually evolving. Startups must ensure compliance with local laws, which can be both costly and time-consuming. Failure to adhere to regulatory requirements can result in legal penalties, impacting the startup's ability to operate and grow. Investors must also stay informed about regulatory developments to understand the potential risks and implications for their investments.

Market volatility is an inherent risk in the cryptocurrency space. The value of digital assets can fluctuate dramatically due to factors such as market sentiment, technological advancements, and regulatory news. This volatility can affect both the funding and operational stability of crypto startups, as well as the value of investments. Effective risk management strategies, including thorough due diligence, diversification, and staying informed about market trends, are essential for navigating this volatility.

The success stories of Bitcoin, Ethereum, Binance, Chainlink, and Uniswap highlight the potential rewards and impact of innovative blockchain projects. These startups have introduced groundbreaking technologies, created new markets, and achieved significant financial success. Their journeys offer valuable lessons for both entrepreneurs and investors in understanding the factors that contribute to success in the crypto space.

For entrepreneurs, success requires a combination of technical expertise, strategic planning, and the ability to adapt to a rapidly changing environment. Building a skilled team, identifying a compelling use case for blockchain technology, and creating a viable product are critical steps. Navigating regulatory challenges and securing sufficient funding are also essential components of a successful startup journey.

For investors, a disciplined and informed approach is key to maximizing returns and managing risks. Conducting thorough research on potential investments, diversifying across multiple projects, and staying informed about regulatory and market developments are crucial strategies. Learning from successful projects and understanding the common pitfalls can help investors make better decisions and achieve more consistent returns.

In conclusion, building and investing in crypto startups offers exciting opportunities for high returns and involvement in cutting-edge technological advancements. However, these ventures come with significant risks that must be carefully managed. By understanding the unique challenges of the blockchain industry, leveraging effective strategies, and learning from successful examples, entrepreneurs and investors can navigate the complexities of this dynamic space. This approach will enable them to contribute to the growth of the blockchain ecosystem and potentially achieve substantial financial rewards, while also driving innovation and transformation across various sectors of the global economy.

Chapter 11: Education and Consulting

Leveraging Knowledge to Educate or Consult

The rapid growth of the cryptocurrency and blockchain industry has created a significant demand for education and consulting services. As the technology continues to evolve and its applications expand, individuals and businesses seek to understand its complexities and harness its potential. Education and consulting in the crypto space involve leveraging deep knowledge and expertise to guide others, whether through formal teaching, workshops, seminars, or one-on-one consulting services. Professionals in this field provide valuable insights into blockchain technology, cryptocurrency trading, regulatory compliance, security practices, and more, helping clients navigate this intricate landscape.

Educators and consultants play a crucial role in demystifying the technology, offering tailored advice, and helping clients implement effective strategies. This can involve developing educational content, conducting training sessions, providing strategic business advice, and assisting with technical implementations. By sharing their expertise, educators and consultants empower others to make informed decisions, drive innovation, and achieve their goals within the crypto and blockchain space.

Advantages

Monetizing Expertise

One of the primary advantages of education and consulting in the cryptocurrency industry is the ability to monetize expertise. Professionals with a deep understanding of blockchain technology and cryptocurrencies can translate their knowledge into lucrative opportunities. As demand for expert advice grows, so does the willingness of individuals and businesses to pay for high-quality education and consulting services. This can result in a steady and substantial income stream for knowledgeable professionals.

Monetizing expertise in this field offers several benefits:

1. **Financial Rewards**: Experts can command high fees for their services, particularly if they have a proven track record of success or a unique specialization. This can lead to significant earnings, especially as the market for crypto education and consulting continues to expand.
2. **Flexibility**: Education and consulting provide flexibility in terms of work arrangements. Professionals can offer their services remotely, in-person, or through a combination of both. This flexibility allows for a better work-life balance and the ability to reach a global audience.
3. **Recognition and Influence**: Establishing oneself as an expert in the crypto space can lead to increased recognition and influence. This can open doors to speaking engagements, media opportunities, and collaboration with industry leaders, further enhancing one's professional reputation and network.

Risks

Requires Deep Understanding and Effective Marketing

While the opportunities in crypto education and consulting are plentiful, they come with significant risks and challenges. One of the main requirements is having a deep and comprehensive understanding of blockchain technology and the cryptocurrency market. This knowledge must be constantly updated, as the industry evolves rapidly with new developments, regulations, and technological advancements.

Educators and consultants must stay abreast of these changes to provide accurate and relevant advice.

Effective marketing is another crucial component. Building a successful education or consulting business requires more than just expertise; it also involves reaching the right audience and effectively communicating the value of one's services. Professionals must develop strong marketing strategies to attract clients, which can include building a personal brand, leveraging social media, creating high-quality content, and networking within the industry.

Other risks include:

1. **Intense Competition**: The growing demand for crypto education and consulting has led to increased competition. Standing out in a crowded market requires not only expertise but also unique selling points and effective differentiation strategies.
2. **Regulatory Uncertainty**: The evolving regulatory landscape for cryptocurrencies can impact education and consulting services. Professionals must ensure they are compliant with relevant laws and regulations to avoid legal issues.
3. **Client Trust and Satisfaction**: Building and maintaining client trust is crucial for long-term success. Delivering high-quality services and achieving positive outcomes for clients is essential to establish a strong reputation and secure repeat business.

Building a Consulting Business

Steps to Establish and Grow

Building a successful consulting business in the cryptocurrency and blockchain space involves several key steps. Here's a detailed guide to establishing and growing your consulting business:

1. **Develop Expertise and Credentials**
    - **Education**: Invest in your education by taking courses, attending workshops, and obtaining relevant certifications in blockchain technology, cryptocurrency trading, and related fields. This foundational knowledge is crucial for establishing credibility.
    - **Experience**: Gain practical experience by working on real-world projects, participating in blockchain communities, and staying actively involved in the industry. Practical experience enhances your understanding and provides valuable insights that can benefit your clients.

1. **Identify Your Niche**
    - **Specialization**: Determine your area of specialization within the crypto space. This could be blockchain development, regulatory compliance, security, trading strategies, or another niche. Specializing allows you to offer targeted services and stand out in the market.
    - **Target Audience**: Identify your target audience, whether it's individual investors, startups, established businesses, or government entities. Understanding your audience's needs helps tailor your services and marketing efforts.

1. **Create a Strong Brand**

- **Brand Identity**: Develop a professional brand identity, including a logo, website, and social media presence. Your brand should reflect your expertise, professionalism, and unique value proposition.
- **Content Marketing**: Create high-quality content that showcases your knowledge and provides value to your audience. This can include blog posts, whitepapers, case studies, videos, and webinars. Content marketing helps establish you as a thought leader and attracts potential clients.

1. **Network and Build Relationships**
   - **Industry Events**: Attend industry conferences, meetups, and networking events to connect with potential clients and other professionals. Networking helps build relationships and opens up opportunities for collaboration and referrals.
   - **Online Communities**: Participate in online communities, such as forums, social media groups, and professional networks. Engaging with these communities can enhance your visibility and credibility within the industry.

1. **Offer Free Initial Consultations**
   - **Consultation**: Offering free initial consultations can help attract clients and demonstrate the value of your services. Use this opportunity to understand their needs, provide valuable insights, and build trust.
   - **Client Testimonials**: Collect and showcase testimonials from satisfied clients. Positive feedback

serves as social proof and can significantly enhance your reputation.

1. **Set Competitive Pricing**
    - **Pricing Strategy**: Develop a competitive pricing strategy based on your expertise, market rates, and the value you provide. Consider offering different pricing tiers or packages to cater to various client needs and budgets.
    - **Value Proposition**: Clearly communicate the value of your services and how they can help clients achieve their goals. A strong value proposition justifies your pricing and encourages clients to invest in your expertise.

1. **Continuously Improve and Adapt**
    - **Feedback**: Regularly seek feedback from clients to understand their satisfaction and areas for improvement. Use this feedback to refine your services and enhance the client experience.
    - **Stay Updated**: Keep up with industry trends, technological advancements, and regulatory changes. Continuous learning ensures that your knowledge remains relevant and valuable to clients.

1. **Expand Your Services**
    - **Additional Services**: As your business grows, consider expanding your service offerings to include workshops, training programs, or online courses. Diversifying your services can increase revenue streams and reach a broader audience.
    - **Partnerships**: Explore partnerships with other

professionals or firms to offer complementary
services and create bundled solutions for clients.

Conclusion

Engaging in education and consulting within the cryptocurrency and blockchain industry presents a unique and lucrative opportunity for professionals to monetize their expertise while contributing to the broader adoption and understanding of these technologies. As the industry continues to evolve and expand, the demand for knowledgeable educators and consultants is only set to increase, offering substantial financial and professional rewards for those who can effectively leverage their skills.

One of the primary advantages of entering the field of crypto education and consulting is the potential for high earnings. By sharing valuable insights and providing expert guidance, professionals can command significant fees for their services. This not only creates a steady income stream but also opens doors to various other opportunities, such as speaking engagements, media appearances, and collaborations with industry leaders. The flexibility associated with consulting and education roles further enhances their appeal, allowing professionals to work remotely and cater to a global client base.

However, the path to success in crypto education and consulting is not without its challenges. A deep and continuously updated understanding of blockchain technology and the cryptocurrency market is essential. The rapid pace of innovation and frequent regulatory changes require professionals to stay informed and adapt their knowledge and strategies accordingly. Additionally, effective marketing is crucial to stand out in a competitive landscape. Building a strong personal brand, creating high-quality content, and networking within the industry are vital steps to attract clients and establish credibility.

The risks associated with this field also include intense competition and the necessity of building and maintaining client trust. Delivering high-quality services and achieving positive outcomes for clients are paramount to securing repeat business and fostering long-term relationships. Moreover, regulatory uncertainties can impact the scope and nature of consulting services, necessitating a thorough understanding of legal requirements and compliance issues.

Despite these challenges, the success stories of various crypto startups underscore the potential impact and rewards of effective education and consulting. By helping individuals and businesses navigate the complexities of blockchain technology and cryptocurrency markets, educators and consultants play a critical role in driving the industry forward. Their contributions not only aid in demystifying the technology but also empower clients to make informed decisions and capitalize on emerging opportunities.

For those looking to build a consulting business in this space, a systematic approach is essential. Developing expertise, identifying a niche, creating a strong brand, networking, offering initial consultations, setting competitive pricing, and continuously improving services are all critical steps to establishing a successful venture. Expanding service offerings and exploring partnerships can further enhance the business's reach and revenue potential.

In summary, the field of crypto education and consulting offers significant opportunities for professionals to leverage their knowledge and expertise for financial gain and industry influence. While the journey involves navigating various risks and challenges, the rewards of contributing to the growth and understanding of blockchain technology are substantial. By remaining informed, adaptable, and client-focused, educators and consultants can build thriving businesses and play a pivotal role in the ongoing evolution of the cryptocurrency landscape.

Conclusions and Summary

Summary of Strategies

1. Buy and Hold (HODL)

- **Description**: Buy and hold is a long-term investment strategy where investors purchase cryptocurrencies and hold onto them for an extended period, regardless of market fluctuations. This approach is based on the belief that, despite short-term volatility, the value of cryptocurrencies will appreciate over time.
- **Advantages**:
    - **Minimal Time Investment**: Requires less frequent monitoring compared to active trading.
    - **Potential for Significant Gains**: Historically, major cryptocurrencies like Bitcoin and Ethereum have shown substantial long-term growth.
- **Risks**:
    - **Market Volatility**: Prices can fluctuate widely in the short term.
    - **Patience Required**: Investors must withstand periods of low or negative returns.

2. Trading Strategies

- **Day Trading**
    - **Description**: Day trading involves buying and selling cryptocurrencies within a single trading day to profit from short-term price movements. Traders capitalize on the market's

volatility by making multiple trades throughout the day.

- ○ **Advantages:**
    - **High Potential for Quick Profits**: Can yield significant returns in a short period.
    - **No Overnight Risk**: Positions are closed by the end of the day.
- ○ **Risks:**
    - **High Risk**: Requires quick decision-making and constant monitoring.
    - **Higher Transaction Fees**: Frequent trading incurs more fees.

- **Swing Trading**
    - ○ **Description**: Swing trading involves holding onto a cryptocurrency for several days to weeks to profit from expected price swings. Traders use technical analysis to identify market trends and potential entry and exit points.
    - ○ **Advantages:**
        - **Balance Between Day Trading and HODLing**: Offers the potential for significant gains without constant monitoring.
        - **Leverages Market Trends**: Can capitalize on both uptrends and downtrends.
    - ○ **Risks:**
        - **Overnight Risks**: Exposure to market changes outside of trading hours.
        - **Requires Market Analysis Skills**: Success depends on the trader's ability to analyze and predict market movements.

- **Technical Analysis**
    - ○ **Description**: Using charts, historical price data, and various technical indicators, traders forecast future price movements to inform their trading decisions.

- ○ **Advantages:**
    - ▪ **Systematic Approach:** Provides a structured method for making trading decisions.
    - ▪ **Helps Identify Trends:** Can reveal patterns and trends that are not immediately apparent.
- ○ **Risks:**
    - ▪ **Historical Data Limitations:** Past performance is not always indicative of future results.
    - ▪ **Complexity:** Requires understanding and interpreting various technical indicators and chart patterns.

3. Staking

- **Description:** Staking involves participating in the validation of transactions on a blockchain network by holding and locking up a specific amount of cryptocurrency. This helps secure the network and earns the staker rewards.
- **Advantages:**
    - ○ **Generates Passive Income:** Earn rewards in the form of additional cryptocurrency.
    - ○ **Supports Network Security:** Contributes to the stability and security of the blockchain network.
- **Risks:**
    - ○ **Coin Value Fluctuation:** The value of staked coins can drop, impacting returns.
    - ○ **Lock-Up Periods:** Staked assets are often locked for a certain period, reducing liquidity.
    - ○ **Liquidity Risks:** Difficulty in accessing staked assets quickly in response to market changes.

4. Yield Farming and Liquidity Mining

- **Description**: Yield farming involves providing liquidity to DeFi (Decentralized Finance) protocols in exchange for rewards, usually in the form of additional tokens. Liquidity mining specifically refers to earning tokens by providing liquidity.
- **Advantages**:
    - **High Returns**: Potentially significant rewards for providing liquidity to high-demand protocols.
    - **Passive Income**: Once liquidity is provided, rewards accrue without active management.
- **Risks**:
    - **Smart Contract Vulnerabilities**: DeFi protocols can have bugs or security flaws.
    - **Impermanent Loss**: Loss incurred when the value of staked tokens changes relative to the initial deposit.

5. Mining

- **Description**: Cryptocurrency mining involves using computational power to solve complex mathematical problems, which validates transactions and adds them to the blockchain. Miners are rewarded with newly created coins.
- **Advantages**:
    - **Earning New Coins**: Generates new cryptocurrency as a reward for mining.
    - **Supports Network Security**: Ensures the integrity and security of the blockchain.
- **Risks**:
    - **High Initial Investment**: Requires significant upfront costs for mining hardware.
    - **Ongoing Costs**: Continuous electricity and maintenance costs.

- ○ **Hardware Obsolescence**: Rapid advancements in technology can make mining hardware outdated.

6. Arbitrage

- **Description**: Arbitrage involves exploiting price differences of a specific cryptocurrency across different exchanges. Traders buy the asset at a lower price on one exchange and sell it at a higher price on another.
- **Advantages**:
  - ○ **Low Risk**: Profits are based on existing price discrepancies, not market predictions.
  - ○ **Quick Profits**: Can generate returns in a short period if executed efficiently.
- **Risks**:
  - ○ **Transfer Times**: Delays in moving assets between exchanges can negate profits.
  - ○ **Transaction Fees**: Fees can erode the small margins typical of arbitrage trades.

7. Airdrops and Forks

- **Description**: Airdrops involve distributing free tokens to cryptocurrency holders, often as part of a marketing strategy. Forks occur when a blockchain splits into two separate chains, resulting in holders receiving new tokens on the forked chain.
- **Advantages**:
  - ○ **Free Assets**: Provides additional tokens without requiring an investment.
  - ○ **Introduces New Projects**: Offers exposure to new cryptocurrencies and projects.

- **Risks**:
  - **Low or Volatile Value**: Airdropped tokens may have little value or be highly volatile.
  - **Scams**: Potential for fraudulent airdrops aimed at stealing private information.

8. Building and Investing in Crypto Startups

- **Description**: Involves developing new blockchain-based projects or investing in startups within the cryptocurrency industry. Entrepreneurs create innovative solutions, while investors provide capital for growth.
- **Advantages**:
  - **High Potential Returns**: Successful startups can generate substantial profits.
  - **Diversification**: Spreading investments across multiple projects reduces risk.
- **Risks**:
  - **High Failure Rate**: Many startups fail to gain traction or become sustainable.
  - **Substantial Investment**: Significant capital is required for development and growth.
  - **Regulatory Uncertainty**: Changing regulations can impact startup operations.

9. Education and Consulting

- **Description**: Leveraging expertise in blockchain and cryptocurrencies to educate others or provide consulting services. This can involve teaching, conducting workshops, or offering strategic advice.
- **Advantages**:

- ○ **Monetizing Expertise**: Earn income by sharing knowledge and providing valuable insights.
  - ○ **Flexibility**: Consulting and education offer flexible work arrangements.
  - ○ **Industry Influence**: Establishes professionals as thought leaders and increases visibility.
- **Risks**:
  - ○ **Requires Deep Understanding**: Continuous learning is necessary to stay current.
  - ○ **Effective Marketing Needed**: Building a client base requires strong marketing efforts.
  - ○ **Client Trust and Satisfaction**: High-quality services are essential to maintaining reputation.

Final Tips

1. **Stay Informed**: Continuously update your knowledge about the cryptocurrency market, technological advancements, and regulatory changes. Subscribing to industry newsletters, following thought leaders on social media, and participating in online forums can help you stay ahead.
2. **Diversify Investments**: Spread your investments across different cryptocurrencies and strategies to mitigate risks and enhance potential returns. Avoid putting all your capital into a single asset or project.
3. **Implement Risk Management**: Always assess and manage the risks associated with each investment. Set stop-loss orders, use appropriate leverage, and only invest money you can afford to lose.
4. **Secure Your Assets**: Use reputable wallets and exchanges, enable two-factor authentication, and be vigilant against phishing scams and other security threats. Consider using

hardware wallets for long-term storage of significant holdings.

5. **Have a Clear Plan**: Define your investment goals, time horizon, and risk tolerance. Develop a strategy that aligns with your objectives and stick to it, avoiding impulsive decisions based on market noise.

6. **Network and Learn from Others**: Engage with the cryptocurrency community through online forums, social media groups, and industry events. Networking can provide valuable insights, opportunities, and support.

7. **Keep Emotions in Check**: The volatile nature of the crypto market can lead to emotional decision-making. Maintain a disciplined approach and avoid making investment decisions based on fear or greed.

Final words

Embarking on your journey in the cryptocurrency market is an exhilarating and transformative experience, full of both challenges and opportunities. The potential for financial growth, technological innovation, and personal development within this space is truly boundless. Remember, every successful investor and entrepreneur began their journey with uncertainties and setbacks. The key to achieving success lies in perseverance, continuous learning, and the courage to adapt and evolve.

The cryptocurrency market is unlike any other. It's a dynamic, ever-changing landscape that offers unparalleled opportunities for those willing to dive in and understand its complexities. The road ahead will not always be smooth. There will be moments of doubt, volatility, and unforeseen challenges. However, these obstacles are also what make the journey so rewarding. Each challenge you face and overcome strengthens your resolve and brings you one step closer to your goals.

As you implement the strategies and insights from this eBook, maintain a mindset of resilience and adaptability. The cryptocurrency market is known for its rapid changes and innovations, which means staying updated and flexible is crucial. Continuous learning is your greatest ally. Immerse yourself in the latest trends, technologies, and market movements. Join communities, participate in discussions, attend webinars, and never hesitate to seek knowledge from various sources. The more informed you are, the better equipped you will be to make strategic decisions.

Remember that every small step you take in the cryptocurrency world is a building block towards your larger goals. Success in this field is not about making quick wins but about steady, informed progress. Each investment, each trade, each new piece of knowledge adds to your overall expertise and brings you closer to mastering the market. It's essential to celebrate these small victories and use them as motivation to keep moving forward.

The potential rewards in the cryptocurrency market are immense, but they require a disciplined and patient approach. Stay motivated by setting clear, achievable goals. Break down your long-term objectives into smaller, manageable tasks. This will not only make your journey less overwhelming but also allow you to track your progress and stay focused. Patience is a virtue in the crypto world, where the market's volatility can test even the most seasoned investors. Trust in your strategies, stay the course, and remember that success often comes to those who are willing to wait.

Moreover, embrace the innovative spirit of the cryptocurrency world. This industry thrives on innovation and disruption. Don't be afraid to explore new ideas, experiment with different strategies, and think outside the box. Your creativity and willingness to innovate can set you apart from others and lead to unique opportunities. The crypto market rewards those who are bold enough to forge their own path and create value in new and unexpected ways.

Networking and community engagement are also vital aspects of your journey. The cryptocurrency community is vibrant and diverse, filled with individuals who share your passion and curiosity. Engage with this community, build connections, and exchange ideas. Networking not only provides valuable insights but also opens doors to new opportunities and collaborations. Surrounding yourself with like-minded individuals can provide support, encouragement, and a wealth of knowledge.

Lastly, maintain a balanced perspective. While it's important to stay focused and dedicated, it's equally crucial to take care of your mental and emotional well-being. The volatility and intensity of the crypto market can be overwhelming at times. Take breaks, manage stress, and ensure you have a support system in place. A clear and calm mind is essential for making sound decisions and navigating the market effectively.

In conclusion, believe in your potential to make informed, strategic decisions. Each step you take, no matter how small, brings you closer to your goals. Embrace the challenges and learn from them, for they are stepping stones to success. The journey may be demanding, but the rewards are well worth the effort. The cryptocurrency market is a dynamic and evolving landscape. Stay adaptable, keep refining your strategies, and continue expanding your knowledge. Your dedication and hard work will pave the way for success in this rapidly growing industry.

Stay confident, stay disciplined, and keep your vision clear. The world of crypto offers limitless possibilities, and with the right mindset and approach, you can achieve remarkable success. Here's to your journey and the exciting opportunities that await you in the cryptocurrency market! Believe in yourself, stay resilient, and let your passion for innovation drive you forward. The future is fruitful, and it's yours to reap.

Additional Resources

To further enhance your understanding and success in the cryptocurrency market, this section provides a comprehensive guide to essential resources. These include a glossary of common terms, suggestions for further reading, and recommendations for useful tools and platforms. Each of these resources will help deepen your knowledge and equip you with the tools needed to navigate the complex world of cryptocurrencies and blockchain technology effectively.

Glossary of Terms

Common Cryptocurrency and Blockchain Terminology

1. **Address**: A unique string of characters used to send and receive cryptocurrency transactions.
2. **Altcoin**: Any cryptocurrency other than Bitcoin. Examples include Ethereum, Ripple (XRP), and Litecoin.
3. **Blockchain**: A decentralized ledger of all transactions across a network. It is maintained by a distributed network of nodes.
4. **Consensus Mechanism**: The process used to achieve agreement on the state of the blockchain. Common types include Proof of Work (PoW) and Proof of Stake (PoS).
5. **Cryptocurrency**: A digital or virtual currency that uses cryptography for security and operates independently of a central authority.
6. **Decentralized Finance (DeFi)**: Financial services using smart contracts on a blockchain, aiming to create a more open, accessible, and transparent financial system.

7. **Ethereum**: A blockchain platform with smart contract functionality, enabling developers to create decentralized applications (dApps).
8. **Fork**: A split in the blockchain where two versions of the ledger emerge, often due to changes in the consensus rules.
9. **Gas**: A fee required to execute transactions or smart contracts on the Ethereum network, paid in Ether (ETH).
10. **Halving**: An event in Bitcoin where the reward for mining new blocks is halved, occurring approximately every four years.
11. **Hash Rate**: The measure of computational power per second used when mining cryptocurrencies.
12. **Initial Coin Offering (ICO)**: A fundraising method where new cryptocurrencies are sold to early investors before being listed on exchanges.
13. **Liquidity**: The ease with which an asset can be bought or sold without affecting its price.
14. **Mining**: The process of using computational power to solve complex problems and validate transactions on a blockchain, earning new coins as a reward.
15. **Node**: A computer that participates in a blockchain network by maintaining a copy of the ledger and validating transactions.
16. **Private Key**: A secret key used to sign transactions and prove ownership of a blockchain address.
17. **Public Key**: A key that is shared publicly and used to receive cryptocurrency.
18. **Smart Contract**: Self-executing contracts with the terms directly written into code, running on a blockchain.
19. **Stablecoin**: A cryptocurrency pegged to a stable asset, such as a fiat currency, to minimize price volatility.
20. **Token**: A digital asset created on an existing blockchain,

representing various forms of value or utility.

21. **Wallet**: A digital tool for storing and managing cryptocurrencies. It can be hardware-based, software-based, or paper-based.

Further Reading: Books, Articles, and Websites for Deeper Understanding

Books:

1. **"Mastering Bitcoin: Unlocking Digital Cryptocurrencies" by Andreas M. Antonopoulos**
   - A comprehensive guide to Bitcoin, covering everything from the basics to advanced concepts.
2. **"Blockchain Basics: A Non-Technical Introduction in 25 Steps" by Daniel Drescher**
   - An accessible introduction to blockchain technology, ideal for beginners.
3. **"The Bitcoin Standard: The Decentralized Alternative to Central Banking" by Saifedean Ammous**
   - Explores the history of money and the potential of Bitcoin as a new monetary system.
4. **"Cryptoassets: The Innovative Investor's Guide to Bitcoin and Beyond" by Chris Burniske and Jack Tatar**
   - Provides investment strategies and insights into various cryptocurrencies and blockchain projects.
5. **"Ethereum: Blockchains, Digital Assets, Smart Contracts, Decentralized Autonomous Organizations" by Henning Diedrich**
   - A detailed exploration of Ethereum and its applications.

Articles:

1. **"Bitcoin: A Peer-to-Peer Electronic Cash System" by Satoshi Nakamoto**
    - The original whitepaper introducing Bitcoin, a must-read for understanding the foundation of cryptocurrencies.
2. **"The Tokenization of Everything" by Andreessen Horowitz**
    - An insightful article on how blockchain technology can tokenize various assets.
3. **"DeFi: The Next Generation of the Crypto Economy" by Binance Research**
    - An in-depth analysis of the decentralized finance ecosystem and its potential impact.

Websites:

1. **CoinDesk (www.coindesk.com[1])**
    - A leading news website covering cryptocurrency, blockchain, and fintech.
2. **CoinTelegraph (www.cointelegraph.com[2])**
    - Another major news outlet providing comprehensive coverage of the cryptocurrency industry.
3. **CryptoCompare (www.cryptocompare.com[3])**
    - A platform offering real-time data, reviews, and comparison tools for various cryptocurrencies and exchanges.
4. **Ethereum.org (www.ethereum.org[4])**

---

1. http://www.coindesk.com

2. http://www.cointelegraph.com

3. http://www.cryptocompare.com

4. http://www.ethereum.org

- The official website of Ethereum, providing resources, documentation, and news about the platform.

5. **Bitcoin.org (www.bitcoin.org[5])**
   - The official website of Bitcoin, offering a wealth of information about the cryptocurrency.

Useful Tools and Platforms: Recommended Exchanges, Wallets, and Analytical Tools

Exchanges:

1. **Binance**
   - One of the largest and most popular cryptocurrency exchanges, offering a wide range of cryptocurrencies and trading pairs, low fees, and advanced trading features.

2. **Coinbase**
   - A user-friendly exchange known for its ease of use, security, and support for major cryptocurrencies. Ideal for beginners.

3. **Kraken**
   - A reputable exchange with a strong emphasis on security, offering a variety of cryptocurrencies, advanced trading tools, and staking services.

4. **Bitfinex**
   - An exchange known for its liquidity, advanced trading options, and margin trading capabilities.

5. **Gemini**
   - A regulated exchange with a focus on security and compliance, offering a secure platform for buying, selling, and storing cryptocurrencies.

---

5. http://www.bitcoin.org

Wallets:

1. **Ledger Nano S/X**
   - Hardware wallets offering top-notch security for storing a wide range of cryptocurrencies.
2. **Trezor**
   - Another highly secure hardware wallet with support for multiple cryptocurrencies and user-friendly features.
3. **Trust Wallet**
   - A mobile wallet known for its ease of use, supporting a wide range of cryptocurrencies and providing access to decentralized applications (dApps).
4. **Exodus**
   - A desktop and mobile wallet with an intuitive interface, built-in exchange, and support for multiple cryptocurrencies.
5. **MyEtherWallet (MEW)**
   - A popular web-based wallet specifically designed for Ethereum and ERC-20 tokens, offering robust security features.

Analytical Tools:

1. **CoinMarketCap**
   - A comprehensive resource for real-time cryptocurrency prices, market capitalization, trading volumes, and historical data.
2. **TradingView**
   - A powerful charting and technical analysis tool, widely used by traders for analyzing price movements and trends.

3. **Glassnode**
    - An on-chain data and intelligence platform providing insights into blockchain metrics and market trends.

4. **CryptoCompare**
    - Offers a range of tools and data for comparing cryptocurrencies, exchanges, and wallets, as well as portfolio tracking features.

5. **Messari**
    - A platform providing detailed research, data, and news on various cryptocurrencies and blockchain projects.